Extreme Snowboarding

Canada's Best Riders

Tom Peacock

OVER
TIME
BOOKS

First printed in 2005 10 9 8 7 6 5 4 3 2 1

Printed in Canada

The Publisher: OverTime Books is an imprint of Éditions de la Montagne Verte

Library and Archives Canada Cataloguing in Publication

Peacock, Tom, 1976–
    Extreme snowboarding : Canada's best riders / Tom Peacock.

Includes bibliographical references.
ISBN-13: 978-0-9737681-1-4
ISBN-10: 0-9737681-1-8

    1. Snowboarders—Canada—Biography. 2. Snowboarding—Canada.
I. Title.

GV857.S57P42 2005   796.939'092'271   C2005-906322-X

Project Director: J. Alexander Poulton
Project Editor: Wendy Pirk
Cover Design: Valentino
Production: Linda Bolger
Cover Image: Courtesy of Corbis
Photos: Every effort has been made to accurately credit the sources of photographs. Any errors or omissions should be directed to the publisher for changes in future editions. Photographs courtesy of Joe Rocca (title page; p. 43; 113); Shaun Hughes (p. 9; 124)); Rube Goldberg (p. 56); Crispin Cannon (p. 64; 78; 81; 87; 133).

PC:P5

Table of Contents

Dedication

To Audrey, the craziest snowboarder
this side of the Rockies.

Acknowledgements

Thanks to all the riders who contributed their stories to this book. Thanks especially to Rube Goldberg for all his help getting everything together. Thanks to all the photographers who sent in their shots. Thanks to Jay Poulton for the opportunity to write this book and for keeping the deadlines nice and tight.

Introduction

I WAS A SKI NUT; DRIVING MY OLD BUICK UP TO THE STONEHAM ski resort near my home in Québec City every chance I got; skiing even when it was cold enough to burn your skin.

I was hooked on skiing and wasn't even willing to give snowboarding a chance. Then I met Yvonne Bernier, who also had a season's pass at Stoneham. We planned to meet the next weekend for a few runs. I was a little surprised when she turned up carrying a Burton snowboard. Until that day, I hadn't really spent much time watching anyone snowboard, and I was impressed by how easy my new friend made it look. Yvonne cruised down the hill with the most nonchalant expression on her face. She was totally, "Whatever," about the whole thing. She looked so cool; I felt like a dinosaur. At the end of the day, Yvonne told me her dad had a snowboard he didn't use much and that I could try it if I wanted to. I hemmed and hawed, but inside I was burning with desire. I had to give it a shot.

A few days later, Yvonne showed up at Stoneham with the extra board. I strapped in at the top of the hill and tried to mimic my friend's relaxed style. It didn't work, but I was able to muscle in a few turns before crashing on my butt. It was 10:00 am. By 6:00 pm, Yvonne had quit and headed inside for hot chocolate. Four hours later, the lift attendant told me it was time for my last run. I could have kept going forever. I had gone from being an avid skier to being a snowboarder, and it had taken exactly 12 hours. There was no looking back. I was completely obsessed from that day on, riding every chance I got.

The next season, I was more than ready to start hitting the jumps. By the time it started to warm up and the snow was getting softer, I was hucking myself over Stoneham's huge spring gap jump, spinning frontside and backside. I was nowhere near as good as half the riders on the hill, but every day I was learning something new, pushing myself as hard as I could.

The following winter, I moved to Whistler to ride the best resort in Canada. I wasn't disappointed. I got to ride almost every day with my new buddy Rube Goldberg (who is featured in this book) and witness from afar the death-defying insanity of local legends like Chris Dimma, Omar Lundie, Martin Gallant, Mike Orr, Chris Brown and many other top riders whose names I didn't catch. That season in Whistler instilled in me a respect and admiration for the riders who were willing to push the limits. Now, 10 years later, it's the same game and the riders continue to push themselves as hard as ever.

The idea behind this book was simple: to collect a bunch of crazy stories from a selection of Canada's top riders in order to provide a picture of what goes on in the snowboarding world. I also wanted to show how snowboarders go from being local heroes to international superstars.

This is by no means a scientific effort; many of the best stories from some of the best riders have yet to be told (Devun Walsh, Mike Michalchuk, Natasza Zurek, Marc Morrisette, J.F. Pelchat, Dennis Bannock, Ken Achenbach, and Alex Warburton, to name a few). It would require the writing of a hundred books to get a complete picture of the Canadian snowboarding scene. Like the movies that drive the sport, this book is merely a sample of what's out there, a small taste of what's happened so far.

Read about snowboarding's leading lady Victoria Jealouse shredding the snowy slopes of Alaska, or Shin Campos dropping one of the biggest cliffs on Whistler and riding away clean. Discover half-pipe hero Justin Lamoureux, whose career is just now coming into focus. Follow new-school sensation Etienne Gilbert's climb to the top, and the ups and downs of Rube Goldberg's topsy-turvy snowboarding career. Marvel at rider Risto Scott's charmed life or Ross Rebagliati's tense moments at the 1998 Olympics, and experience a heart-wrenching first-hand account of an avalanche tragedy. Read about near misses and spectacular crashes, incredible victories and heartbreaking defeats. It's all here in this collection of Canada's most extreme snowboarding stories. Happy reading!

ᨏᨎᏇᏇᎧᨏ

CHAPTER ONE

Kevin Sansalone: The Making of a Pro Snowboarder

Do or Die

THE RAIN POUNDED DOWN ON THE RIDERS' TENT. IT WOULDN'T let up. The riders were soaked, but they were pumped, and the huge crowd several hundred yards down the slope was stoked as well. After all,

Kevin Sansalone drops though the trees on a heavy snow day at Callahan Lake, Whistler.

this wasn't just any competition; it was the 1998 Westbeach Classic, the biggest snowboarding event of the year. There were thousands of young people crowded into the base area, dancing around, throwing plastic cups and snowballs at the judges' stand, and cheering like mad for every jumper. Of course, they reserved their loudest screams for the hometown heroes.

One of the jumpers, Kevin Sansalone wasn't supposed to be competing. He hadn't even been invited. It was thanks to his own stubbornness that he was now standing at the top of the hill, strapped to his board. He'd made it happen, and now it was time for him to throw down.

He stood in his bindings, listening to the rain, trying to calm his nerves. He'd already landed some jumps, and he was riding well. The conditions weren't bothering him much, either—just before the contest, Johnny Q had tuned the base of his board, adding texture to give him more speed in the sticky corn snow than most of the other riders. Now all he had to do was stick this one last jump. He'd come this far. Could he do it?

Pounding bass beats shook the slope below where the riders waited for their turn to hit the jump. In the waiting area, they laughed and joked with their friends, pretending the $15,000 in prize money didn't matter to them, even though everyone knew it was still anybody's night.

In Kevin's mind, it was bigger than just the contest. He'd dedicated the last 10 years of his life to snowboarding. There'd been a lot of good times and a lot of successes but a lot of down time too. Had he taken his best shot? Was he done? He hadn't had a board sponsor all season. Was it time to move on and try something else?

He shook his head. No, the time was now. A switch backside rodeo—a trick he'd learned only a few weeks ago in the Mount Seymour backcountry—would do it. It was time to stop thinking, time to go into autopilot. It was do or die time.

"You ready, Kev?" asked the official standing at the top of the hill.

"Yup." Kevin adjusted his goggles one last time, and gave them a quick wipe with the side of his glove. Someone behind him cheered him on, but he didn't turn around. He was focused now on the task at hand. He pointed his board towards the bottom of the hill, and as though it had a will of its own, his board leapt down the slope towards the kicker.

"He's dropping in switch," the announcer said.

"Switch rodeo, switch rodeo," Kevin's mind told his muscles, preparing them to launch him off the jump backwards.

Point it, he told himself, resisting the urge to check his speed. The jump loomed larger, and the music and cheering rushed up towards him, growing louder and louder. For that split second, just before he shot into the air and the experience of 10 years of jumps took over, Kevin had no way of knowing how it was all going to go down.

Skateboard Decks and Edgeless Wrecks

Kevin Sansalone was born into a Catholic-Italian family in North Vancouver, BC, on July 3, 1975. He was a kid with convictions, an altar boy, attending church three days a week. At one point, he even considered becoming a priest. That was before he discovered snowboarding.

Kevin and his friends were heading into grade eight, making the big leap from junior high to high school, and they knew they needed to get serious about something—something new, something different and something where they could meet new friends. At that time, snowboarding wasn't even allowed at Mount Seymour, the local ski hill located practically in the Sansalone's front yard. So Kevin and his friends decided to become (gasp!) skiers.

Before they went down that road though, one of the group, Christos Obretenov, bought a snowboard from Zeller's—a Black Snow. "You're stupid. You're not even allowed on the mountain with that thing," Kevin and his friends told Christos. But he ignored his friends' jibes. He knew he had the best toy in the neighbourhood, and when the snow fell, his friends would all want to try it.

As it turned out, Christos had good timing. That year, Mt. Seymour started allowing snowboards on the hill. Kevin and his other friends abandoned their two-planked plans and raced off to get their own Black Snows. Kevin was hooked on snowboarding from his first day sliding sideways down Mt. Seymour. Soon he was boldly shooting off the chairlift, and charging down the hill hitting every little jump in sight, plastic bags over his boots, his lunch crammed into a hip pack and his crummy ski jacket flapping in the wind.

Before long, snowboarding took over. It absorbed Kevin's life. Every textbook and piece of paper on his desk displayed drawings of snowboarders, and every project he turned in for each of his classes had to do with snowboarding. By the time the next season rolled around, he knew he had to invest some money in some better equipment.

The first good board he bought was a Gnu Chaos. It was an awesome little board, only 143 cm long, with a centred stance and a good tail. Before long, Kevin was doing method airs and hand plants just like his hero, Craig Kelly. Mount Seymour effectively became Kevin's second home. Every day after school, he and his friends would head up to Seymour to ride under the lights. They also entered their first contest that year, a banked slalom race. The race wound through a gully underneath one of the chairlifts on Seymour. Kevin decided just to have fun and not take the race too seriously, but he placed well. As it turned out, that was only the beginning.

The Seymour Kid (Attitude is Everything)

"We were definitely, like, these total punks," says Kevin remembering the next few seasons, when he and his friends began entering every snowboard contest they could find and placing consistently at the top of the field.

"People started calling us the Seymour Kids in Grade 10," Kevin remembers. "Me, Swaro Doven and Derek Scott got first, second and third at every contest we'd show up to. So then, when we started showing up at contests, people were like, 'Oh, those are the Seymour Kids.' That's how it started." Kevin, Derek, Swaro and whoever else happened to be hanging around them at the time soon gained notoriety for their reckless behaviour on and off the slopes, but they were getting noticed for their riding, as well.

Kevin soon picked up his first sponsorship, from the Deep Cove Bike Shop. They gave him some equipment and sent him to snowboard summer camp on the Blackcomb Glacier to learn from the best—Canadian legends like Sean Kearns and Alex Warburton. It was enough to make an adolescent's head spin, *and* get a little swollen.

Before finishing high school, Kevin secured a sponsorship deal with board manufacturer Santa Cruz. His head was growing immense.

"I was getting paid to snowboard, so I just thought I was the coolest kid in the world, or something," Kevin remembers, laughing. "It's funny, though, because looking back, snowboarding and skateboarding weren't even cool yet."

Kevin missed a lot of classes during his last year of high school; he was travelling all over the country to compete. Still, he managed to graduate with honours, a feat he attributes to the fact that he did little else but snowboard and study.

When Kevin finished school, his mother told him he had to either go to school or get a real job. He checked out some colleges but wasn't ready for more school, so he decided to join the workforce. He got a job at Cypress Mountain Sports, a new shop opening up that catered to snowboarders and cross-country skiers.

On Kevin's first day the boss was onto him. "I know you're a pro snowboarder," he said, "but you're not going to run off and quit as soon as it starts snowing, are you?"

"Oh, no," Kevin said, rather half-heartedly, looking around at the boxes of skis and boards and wondering how he was going to manage a whole season of outfitting people with winter gear when his friends were up on the mountain riding. Still, Kevin had inherited a strong work ethic from his Italian father, who had worked hard to provide for his family, so he quit thinking about it and got to work. Then it started snowing.

The first and only "real" job Kevin Sansalone ever had lasted a scant few months. The pull of the mountains was too strong, and before he knew it, he was back on the hill doing what he did best—riding his snowboard.

What followed was several years of riding hard, travelling, filming, competing and even a little bit of college, where Kevin studied sports medicine during the off-season. Through it all, Santa Cruz was Kevin's main sponsor.

"Santa Cruz was really good to me. They took me everywhere. I went to Europe a lot, because they were really big in Europe. That was really cool. Also, they were based in California, so I would go down to Tahoe a bunch."

Closer to home, Kevin began filming with Sean Johnson and Sean Kearns, the legends of Canadian snowboard filmmaking behind the *Whiskey* movies. Kearns had helped Kevin get sponsored, and he used this fact to push his young protégé to go bigger and ride harder.

"After Kevin started getting a little bit of attention, Kearns kind of took him under his wing, and then eventually turned him into a punching bag," remembers professional snowboard photographer Dano Pendygrasse, who would often follow the *Whiskey* film crew to get still shots.

Kevin got a lot of abuse from the *Whiskey* guys, Dano remembers, because a lot of the time, he just didn't seem to get it.

"He was really selfish. He was the guy who would never share his food or whatever. We were just like, 'Listen, buddy. That's not how it works. We're all in this together, and if you don't figure that out, you're not going to make it. He claims that it made a huge impression on him. And I have to say, there's been instances since where he's been really, really generous, but there's still some old Sansalone in there."

Despite the pranks and occasional pitfalls of the snowboarding lifestyle, Kevin's career was rolling along smoothly, and he was quickly establishing himself as one of Canada's gnarliest riders. Then disaster struck.

A Jump Too Far

Kevin and his riding buddy, Devun Walsh, were out in the Seymour backcountry, their usual stomping grounds, with Dano and the *Whiskey* film crew. The jump was nothing they hadn't seen before, but as usual, they were upping the ante, going bigger and farther each time they hit it.

The session was nearing its end and the light was fading, but Devun and Kevin were still charging it. It was Kevin's turn. He bombed down the takeoff, going faster this time than he had all day. His friends shouted encouragement, and Dano readied his camera. The light was right, and Dano knew this jump might yield the shot he needed to make the day worthwhile.

Kevin launched off the jump and soared, spinning slightly inverted. Dano followed him with his lens, his shutter clicking away to get the sequence, but when he realized where Kevin was going to land, his finger eased off the shutter release. Kevin missed his intended landing spot by three metres and came crashing down hard. Everyone heard the sickening crack of bones and wood meeting. Kevin had landed directly on a hidden stump. His friends ran over to where he lay, obviously in tremendous pain and struggling for breath. While the others stood in shock, Kevin looked at Devun, the only one carrying a cellphone.

"Get your phone out; I'm gonna need an airlift!" he managed through gritted teeth.

"Where does it hurt?" someone asked. Kevin didn't answer. He lay still, assessing the situation. He could feel the muscles in his arms and legs cramping as the blood rushed to protect his damaged internal organs. He knew he was in trouble. A quarter of an hour passed, and the throbbing pain grew worse. The cramping in his muscles started to give way to numbness. Lying there in the snow, far from the patrolled slopes, Kevin knew he had to trust his friends to help him get through this.

Devun was back on the phone, shouting now, trying to convince someone they needed help fast. Kevin couldn't feel his arms and legs. He told the others to massage his limbs so he wouldn't lose circulation. They reached under the jackets they had wrapped around him and began vigorously rubbing his arms and legs. Soon, Kevin began to feel the blood moving back through his veins, and the cramping lessened. Still, the pain in his abdomen was excruci-ating, and it was all he could do to keep breathing.

Meanwhile, the sun was slipping behind the trees, and the temperature was dropping. Still, the friends waited.

"Guys, he's not breathing!" Dano shouted after a whole hour had passed. "Come on, Kevin! BREATHE, MAN!" he shouted, turning his friend's head to face him. Kevin was barely conscious, but he managed a laboured breath. There was a long pause, then another breath.

Three more hours passed before the helicopter arrived. In the meantime, Kevin's friends stuck by him. Dano remembers those long hours, silent except for the terrible sound of Kevin's laboured breathing. "I remember holding his hand and every minute or so reminding him to breathe. Every so often, he just kind of stopped. It was pretty hectic, and there were some scary moments when the gurgling from his lungs would stop."

Finally, the rescue team arrived and airlifted Kevin to a hospital. He had broken five ribs off his spine, and his number-seven rib had shattered and punctured his lung.

"It took me three months to be fully recovered," Kevin said. "It happened in the spring, so I was back riding at summer camp on the Blackcomb Glacier."

After the accident, Kevin went right out and got his Avalanche One and Wilderness First Aid certification. "It just made me respect my life a lot more," he said at the time.

He wasn't the only one. "After that, I think everybody got a small cellphone right away, so we could be in contact," Dano remembers. "Beyond that, we all carry first aid kits and ropes on our sleds now. And we always carry satellite phones if we're going really far out."

While the accident may have made Kevin think twice about hucking himself off jumps with sketchy landings, it didn't slow down his snowboarding. In fact, it was after the crash that Kevin's snowboarding really began to take off. He decided to make the big move to the centre of the Canadian snowboarding world—Whistler, BC.

Whistler or Bust

Kevin remembers his decision to move to Whistler. "All the original Seymour Kids just weren't as into riding anymore," he remembers. "I was still way, way into it. And I realized, well, I can either just chill out here in Vancouver, where the seasons are way shorter and the guys aren't into it as much anymore, or I can move to Whistler. And then I realized, you know what? I'm gonna do it."

Kevin realized he had to go for it; he had to change up his scene and meet new people. He wanted to ride with the best Canadian snowboarders of the day, people like Kevin Young and Chris

Brown, so he would be inspired to ride better, more aggressively. "Those guys were all up in Whistler, and it was just the place for me to be."

With the way things were going in snowboarding, it wasn't enough, though, to just move to Whistler and ride the hill, even though it's rated among the best resorts in the world; you still had to travel far and wide in search of fame and glory.

Shortly after moving to Whistler, Kevin decided to ditch his sponsor. They had refused to give him a raise, and they weren't helping him get into any big contests. He entered the 1997–98 season without a board sponsor but still managed to put together a heavy season of travelling and competing.

Soon it was April and the season was winding down, but there was still one big weekend of competitions at Whistler—the World Ski and Snowboard Festival. Kevin flew home with the express goal of finding a board sponsor that would help him get to bigger contests and make his mark on the snowboard world.

Kevin's friend, Jeff Keetley, one of the original Seymour Kids and a talented snowboarder in his own right, was visiting. The two friends decided to take a shot at the weekend's half-pipe contest. The Friday afternoon qualifier was a jam format, with only the best runs counting. Kevin rode hard; he'd given his life over to snowboarding, and he wanted to show his friend what could come with a little sacrifice. Unfortunately, it wasn't meant to happen that way; Jeff made the finals, and Kevin was out.

Kevin hid his disappointment well until he was home alone. He stood in front of the mirror in the bathroom and admonished himself for cracking under the pressure when it mattered most.

"You can't even *qualify*, let alone get to the finals," he said to his reflection, shaking his head. "You're a loser, Kevin."

He looked down at his hands gripping the edge of the grimy sink and went quiet. He stayed like that for several minutes before looking up again at himself in the mirror. In those few moments, peering into his own eyes, something changed inside Kevin. Self-pity gave way to determination.

He knew what he needed to do.

A Chance

In Whistler, the next day dawned with a sky that looked like a dirty dishrag; thick clouds obscured the surrounding peaks, and steady rain poured down on the few brave souls wandering around the village. Rain or shine, the Westbeach Snowboard Shop and Apparel company was hosting the "Westbeach Classic," the World Ski and Snowboard Festival's Big Air contest, at the bottom of the hill that night, and an air of anticipation hung over the slushy base area.

Kevin hadn't been invited, but he headed down to the site that afternoon, determined to be a contender. He strode right up to the registration table in the lodge, and without even introducing himself, demanded to be put on the list.

"You've gotta let me in," he insisted.

"Sorry, it's invite only, and we don't have any more spots," the official said, without looking up from his computer. Kevin asked him again, and again the official shook his head without looking up.

This went on for several minutes until the official got snippy and told him to forget it; he wasn't going to jump that night. Kevin sat down in a chair by the far wall. He wasn't giving up. After a while, his friend, fellow rider Mike Page, also showed up and asked to be put on the list, but he got the same response.

The start of the contest loomed closer and closer. Riders were warming up on the jump. Watching them through the window of the lodge, Kevin felt like a kid in detention. Why wouldn't they just let him go up there and prove himself? If he did, he'd silence the doubters soon enough; he'd show them he belonged there, among the best.

This sucks, he thought. *There must be someone I can—*

His thoughts were cut off by the official's voice. "Hey, you guys. Kevin, Mike, get over here." The official was waving his hand, motioning for them to come over to the table. The two riders jumped up and made their way over to him, trying not to run. The official was holding a telephone in one hand and a pen in the other.

"Kevin Young and Chris are a scratch. You guys are in, okay? But don't make a lot of noise about it."

For a moment, Kevin didn't say anything. He just looked out of the window at the jump. It was still raining, and the sky was getting dark, but Kevin felt like he'd never seen a more beautiful sight than that soggy mound of snow waiting under the lights. Without a word, he grabbed his board—a blank one he'd gotten from his new friends at Option Snowboards in Vancouver—and strode towards the door.

"Wait, Kevin." Kevin turned around. "You've still gotta fill in the paperwork," the official said smiling.

One Last Jump

Kevin's friend, Johnny Q, board designer for Option, was standing over Kevin, who was undoing his bindings in the landing area. Kevin explained what had happened.

"That's awesome, man!"

"I know, I know. But the conditions are lousy. I can hardly get over the jump. The snow is super sticky."

"Give me your board." Kevin handed it over. "I'll be back in five." Johnny ran off with the board, and true to his word, he came back in a matter of minutes.

"What did you do to it?"

"Just try it," Johnny said.

A few minutes later, Kevin strapped in at the top of the hill and pointed his board down towards the jump. "Holy..." he whispered under his breath. "I'm flying."

Flying he was. Kevin soared over the jump with ease, and as the contest got under way, he continued what amounted to a spectacle of complete and total domination, landing almost every trick he tried.

Finally, it was time for his last judged jump.

"He's dropping in switch, folks," the announcer said. "That's backwards, for all of you fans who don't know the lingo."

Kevin tore down the run, crouching low as he approached the lip of the jump. "Switch rodeo, switch rodeo," he told himself, mentally and physically preparing himself for the maneuver. A split second later, he sprung into the air off his heels and soared over the flat top of the jump, spinning upside down. The crowd paused for a moment, heads craned upwards, waiting to see what was going to happen. It looked like chaos. Could he possibly land such a huge jump? Or was it going to be the night's most spectacular crash?

But Kevin came smoking back to earth like a cat, landing solidly on his feet. He raised his hands over his head, and the crowd went nuts, knowing one of their own was now in the running for first place.

"Kevin Sansalone, ladies and gentlemen!" the announcer shouted into the microphone. "Kevin

SANSALONE with a Switch Rodeo. This could be it, folks. This…COULD…BE…IT!"

In the end, that *was* it; Kevin had shown the doubters. At the end of the day, after not having even been invited, he had come out ready to play and ended up at the top of the heap.

That night, he also ended up securing a board sponsorship from Option.

"Right there on stage, the Option team manager had a sweatshirt for me," he remembers. "It was cool. I said, if you can get me to the X-games, I'll ride for Option."

More Than a Flash in the Pan

The following year, Kevin went to the X-Games, where he won another gold medal in the Big Air Event. The year after that, he won gold again at the Westbeach Classic, and silver at the Gravity Games, another giant extreme contest televised around the world. With those contest results and plenty of coverage in the magazines and videos, Kevin established himself as one of Canada's biggest snowboarding stars. Now, several years later, he's still riding hard, but he's spending more time now helping younger riders come up.

Gone is the selfish little snowboarder of yore, replaced by a benevolent superstar who cares about the community that gave him so much. "We're in the Mecca of snowboarding here [in Whistler] and there are a lot of opportunities here for people to help a lot of other people out," he says.

Kevin is following in the footsteps of his *Whiskey* mentors, making snowboard movies featuring the hottest young talents in Canadian riding; guys like Simon Chamberlain, Dustin Craven and Scott Shaw. His production company, aptly named Skids Productions (a reference to his roots as a Seymour Kid) operates out of his own home. He has already released four movies and is working on his fifth at the time this book is being written.

"We film, film and film all season, and then we make the movie in like, two months," he says. "Those last two months are just hell. The guys come in, and we go through their stuff. I pick what I like, and they pick what they like, and we make a part together. Then we put some music to it. It's hell for a couple of months, and then it goes back to normal."

Normal? Yeah, right…

CHAPTER TWO

Victoria Jealouse: Canada's Queen of Extreme

Riding on the Edge

A DEEP, DRAWN OUT RUMBLING SOUND FILLED THE AIR.

Victoria's blood went cold. She knew that sound. Avalanche.

From her viewpoint near the mountain top, she hadn't seen anything, but she'd grown up in the mountains; she knew what a thousand tons of snow setting off like a freight train down the side of a mountain sounded like. She grabbed her radio.

"Guys, what's happening down there?"

A voice came back, loud but incoherent, over the walkie-talkie. Victoria pressed the button on her radio again.

"What? What did you say? Listen, I can't hear you." Suddenly Victoria felt more alone than she'd ever felt. She had spent the last few years living out of a suitcase, racing her snowboard in dozens of countries where she didn't know a soul, but nothing compared to being alone at the top of that snowy slope in Alaska.

Victoria looked up to where she and Dave Hatchett had ridden over the ridge, down to where she now waited. Dave had ridden on ahead, disappearing over the blind roll in front of her. Had he triggered the avalanche? It didn't matter; there was no going back. Turning around and trudging back up the mountain would be even more difficult and dangerous than going down. Eventually she was going to have to point her board over the blind roll and ride to the bottom.

"...Avalanche," the voice on the radio said. "Dave is—KKHHHHHH...." The static kicked in.

"What? I can't...Is Dave all right?" Victoria said into her radio. There was a long pause. She waited, trying not to let panic set in.

"The slope ripped, but he's okay."

"What about my line?" Victoria asked.

There was another pause. "Victoria, you're going to have to go for it. The snow might go, so ride as fast as you can and try to stay out of it."

Victoria turned off her radio and put it back in her jacket pocket. She double-checked her avalanche transceiver. Everything was ready; now she just had to convince her mind to let go.

She'd seen Dave's line from the helicopter and knew that if the slope had avalanched, she was going to be riding down on hang-fire snow. She had to drop in, even though she knew her chances of setting off a slide were as good as it gets. If the snow did slide, she might very well find herself tumbling uncontrollably towards a snowy grave.

What did I sign on for? she wondered. Mike McEntire (aka Mack Dawg) and Dave Hatchett's brother, Mike, from Standard Films were at the bottom of the slope hoping to get a good shot of her as she came over the blind roll onto the snow-field. Victoria didn't want her first time riding with a film crew to be her last day alive.

She levered herself to a standing position on the steep slope and turned her board at a slight angle to the fall line. As she started to move down the slope, her riding instinct took over. She eased into a toe-side turn, dragging her glove over the pow-dery surface of the snow. Before long, she was approaching the blind roll down onto the steep snowfield. "Gently, gently," she said to herself, and with a long heel-side turn, she was over the hump and riding down the steep wide-open face of the mountain. What seemed like miles below her, she could just make out the black spots that were the film crew. Off to the right, she saw a huge off-white patch where the slope had slid. A chunky mess of debris fanned out in a half circle below it.

Victoria tore down the face, measuring her turns to just skim the surface and desperately trying not to disrupt the snow pack. Soon, she was near enough to the bottom to hear her friends' screams of encouragement.

Almost as soon as it had started, the run was over, and Victoria was undoing her bindings out of harm's way. "That was awesome!" shouted Dave, running over to where she was lying on her back in the deep snow, breathing hard. "You were going SOOOO FAST down that!"

Victoria looked up at her friend and smiled. All in a day's work.

One Fateful Turn

Kamloops, BC native Victoria Jealouse was skiing on the Blackcomb Glacier one day during the summer of 1989 when a friend asked her to try snowboarding. Ski racing had been her life up until that point. She was on the Canadian development team, and she had never even considered snowboarding as an option. Still, her friend insisted.

A few minutes later, Victoria found herself strapped to a snowboard, staring down the glacier, wondering what she had gotten herself into.

She planted her hands in the snow beside her and popped to her feet. "That was easy enough," she said. "Now, I've just gotta turn." She swung her shoulders sideways, and the board turned towards the bottom of the hill. Very soon, she started picking up speed. She leaned forward, and the board arced through a perfect toe-side turn. "Now the other way," she said. She tried to swing the board into a heel-side, it refused to cooperate. She looked down the hill in the direction she was headed, and the next thing she knew, she was flat on her back in the snow.

"Hey Vic! You, okay?" her friend asked, skiing down towards her.

"Yeah. I'm fine." She hadn't hurt herself, but something inside her had been disrupted; not by the fall, but by the turn that had preceded it; that perfect arcing carve—the kind of turn that had taken her years to perfect on skis. Victoria looked down at the board on her feet, and she knew right then that everything had changed. Her life had just gotten knocked sideways by one perfect turn.

For the rest of that summer, Victoria rode her friend's snowboard whenever she could, but she continued her ski training, concealing her new passion from her teammates. The following winter, she continued to race her skis, but whenever she had a chance, she ran the gates on her snowboard, finishing, more often than not, with a spectacular crash.

She was fast on the board, but she couldn't make it very far on the course. Her board would get stuck in a deep carve, and she couldn't reign it in. After a while, though, her years of training as a skier and her natural athleticism rewarded her with a successful run through the gates on her board. With that, she gave up her ski racing entirely and decided to focus on snowboarding.

Victoria had no idea at the time that she was on track to become one of the worlds' most famous big-mountain snowboarders. Her strength had been ski racing, so she decided her best chance of succeeding as a professional snowboarder would be as a racer, not as a free-rider.

"I wanted to be pro because I wanted to snowboard for free," she says now, looking back. "That was my main deal. I wanted to do it as much as I could. That's why I went into racing; because I thought, since I was a ski racer, if I put all my eggs in one basket, at least maybe I would do pretty well. I figured I would probably get a sponsorship sooner or later so I could afford to do it."

A Snowboard Racer, but not for Long

By 1991, Victoria was ready to take on the world. So, without any official sponsor, she packed her boards, withdrew her meagre savings and jumped on a plane to Europe. Her goal was to compete in as many World Cup races as possible before her money ran out.

Race after race, she crashed, and before long, she was running out of money. Then, right when she thought she was going to have to go home, she got a third-place finish at a race in Austria. With that result, her confidence grew. The next race, she got second, and the race after that, she won.

Soon, the people at Burton, the world's most prestigious snowboarding company, took notice of Victoria, and before she had time to say, "I knew I could do it," she was on the team. She still rides for Burton to this day.

The racing continued at a hectic pace for several years, but with each passing season, Victoria focused more and more on free-riding, and she began to distinguish herself as a stylish and daring all-mountain rider. Still, in spite of her ability and guts, she wasn't interested in competing in freestyle events—the most common way for riders to get noticed and invited to free-ride for videos and magazine stories.

"I liked riding half-pipe, but I just didn't want to subject myself to judging," she recalls. "Racing is clean that way. You can flail if you want, and look crazy, but if you go fastest, you win."

Victoria attracted the attention of the free-riding community in spite of herself, and she was invited on a summer trip down to Argentina to shoot photographs with some of the world's current top riders. During that trip, *Transworld Snowboarding* magazine photographer Mark Gallup shot a photograph of Victoria riding through some trees in the fog.

It was the first time the rapidly expanding world of snowboarding was exposed to the name Victoria Jealouse, a name that would crop up hundreds of more times over the years to come, under some of the most iconic images in snowboarding.

The terrain in Mark Gallup's photograph was exotic. It captured the feeling of snowboarding in a strange land. At that time, the early 1990s, the sport of snowboarding was still new, and photographers were just as excited to show riders in strange places as they were to show riders doing crazy jumps or lines.

The photographers weren't beholden to almost two decades of insane snowboard photography, as they are now. They didn't have to consult huge archives to make sure a similar shot hadn't run before.

"Anything you did on your snowboard that was captured in a cool photo got published," Victoria says. It only made sense that if the photographers had more freedom during the sport's early days, then so did the snowboarders. This freedom suited Victoria just fine. After that first trip, Victoria began to see a future in free-riding, and she travelled all over the world to ride.

"Snowboarding is still growing, but not at the crazy exponential rate it was back then. Now they have to run a tight ship, and it has to work, just like anything. Back then, it was growing so fast, your sponsors would just say, here's a bunch of money to go travelling. If at the end of the season they saw you in some magazines, or in a film, or whatever, they were happy. There wasn't anyone keeping track of who did what and for how much."

The Southern Hemisphere was a great place to go and spend other people's money during the summer, but the destination of choice for every major snowboarding crew soon became Alaska. Alaska was in a class by itself. In Alaska, far from the rules and regulations of North American ski resorts, far from the crowds of admiring fans and far from the responsibilities of friends and family, elite riders could get on with the business of surfing mountains.

Alaskan Freedom

Victoria instantly fell in love with the freedom of riding big mountains in Alaska. It suited her personality far more than the structured world of ski racing, or even snowboard racing, for that matter. In Alaska, she could ride what she wanted when she wanted; she just had to find a free seat on the helicopter parked outside the lodge or, if that was full, on the plane that would fly her up to the nearby glacier for $25.

Most of the time, it didn't matter if the riders got any photographs or film footage, as long as they came back with something at the end of the trip. Victoria and her riding friends (Tom Burt, Noah Salasnek, Morgan Lafonte, Mike Devenport, Shawn Farmer, Rocket Reaves or whoever else happened to be around at the time) would hit new mountains every day.

"You could ride forever, probably, and just do first descents all day long if you had enough money to keep the heli in the air," said Mike Devenport in one of the legendary movies of the era, Standard Films' *Coming Down the Mountain*.

There were no guides and no rules to keep the snowboarders in check, just a gun-toting, slightly-crazy-but-gifted helicopter pilot named Chet Simmons, who was more than willing to dump the riders on any peaks that they chose.

"Chet was this crazy good friend of ours, but he was definitely crazy," Victoria recalls. "He'd been shot down maybe 14 times or something in Vietnam and survived. He was all into taking us and landing us on the backsides of cornices and other really weird spots."

The riders spent their days finding new lines that had never been ridden, and hoping they had enough common sense to make it home alive at the end of the day.

"My first trip to Alaska was definitely crazy," Victoria remembers. "Somebody would just be like, 'Hey, the helicopter's coming back. Wanna go up?' And we'd just be like, 'Okay'."

It was a new world, a crazy one full of awesome riders who Victoria wanted to follow down slopes she'd never otherwise attempt, to push the limits of her sport. She wanted to trust them, but she knew she had to be careful. She knew, in the end, the only person she would really be able to trust was herself.

Caught in a Slide

No matter how much you try to be safe, in a place like Alaska, danger always catches up to you. "I saw so many close calls, it was crazy," Victoria says, remembering her earliest trips to the untamed northwest corner of the continent. "There were so many times where I just didn't know how everyone made it through the day. I saw people fall in crevasses and almost stay the night. I saw people walking out on cornices [hanging snow formations, created by wind] that collapsed and going for huge rides."

One thing Victoria never saw, thankfully, was somebody buried alive by an avalanche. She dug out a few partial burials, but the mountains were kind to her and her friends. One day, however, Victoria got caught in a slide herself, and it nearly killed her. It was in the same region as her first trip, around Valdez, Alaska, and she was riding with two big-mountain riding legends—Tom Burt, and Mike Devenport.

The three daredevils were riding huge snow faces that dropped into steep gullies, or couloirs, that spat them out on the lower slopes of the mountain. Mistakes on the upper slopes may have proven fatal—the steep gullies were full of bone crushing rock spires.

When it was Victoria's turn to go, she swooped down the steep upper snow face, slashing the long, carving turns that had become her trademark. Suddenly, the snow under her board began to move, and she knew she was in for it. She steered her board towards the side of the snow face, but it was too late; the snow began to crash down all around her. She lost her balance and began tumbling down in the middle of the slide. The snow picked up momentum heading down to where it would funnel around a corner and into the tight couloir Victoria had hoped to ride down. She fought against the snow as it carried her towards certain death, but it was no use, she couldn't get her board underneath her. Then, just as the snow reached the corner, it spat her out to the side, and she was safe.

"If I hadn't have gotten out of that slide right where I did, I don't think I would have survived it," she says. "Not because it was so big or deep, but because of the exposure. A 300-metre long, narrow couloir with rocks sticking up is something you have to ride down. You can't fall or slide down it, especially if the slide you're stuck in is going about 80 kilometres an hour down there."

Mendenhall Madness

It takes nerves of iron and legs of steel to ride the big mountains of Alaska, but anyone who ever gets a taste of it inevitably wants to go back. Victoria is no exception. She has been going back to Alaska every year since that first trip. During one of her return voyages, she was presented with the chance to follow Dave Hatchett down a line that would cement her place among the best big-mountain riders of all time.

Cascading over a blind roll and down the impossibly steep side of one of the seven jagged Mendenhall Towers that jut out above the Mendenhall Glacier just outside Juneau, Alaska, the line careens down towards a 90-metre monster cliff. A wrong move on the upper part would prove fatal. The fun doesn't end there though; the line then descends past the cliff and over a giant bergschrund—the gap formed when a glacier moves away from a mountainside.

Victoria and the crew flew up to check out the run. "As I was contemplating the first descent of the Mendenhall Towers, there was a lot of negative feedback from the guys I was with," Dave Hatchett said in *Coming Down the Mountain*. "No one really thought it was doable; I knew the snow was good. So I went to the top, and I dropped in."

As Dave dropped in over the blind roll, Victoria watched him go. Would he start a slide? Would he make it past the cliff? Would he fall into the bergschrund? Anything could happen. Luckily, the snow held, and Dave made the historic descent.

Shortly after, the rest of the crew flew up to ride the Towers.

"It was a no-fall zone," Victoria remembers. "Also, if you got caught in your sluff, or if the snow fractured, you wouldn't survive."

Victoria was confident she could ride the exposed slope though, and the snow had held so far. "Once there's a track on it and it doesn't slide, that doesn't mean it's not going to slide, but the percentage goes down a fair amount. Once one person hits it, you know it's not just ready to go. You know it's not super sensitive."

She dropped in. "It was a big face," she remembers, "and you get going super fast, catching air in your turns." Before she knew it, she was off the dangerous, rippled upper slope and heading straight for the 90-metre cliff. The fall line swung to the left, down past the cliff. To avoid going off it, Victoria had to make sure she stayed in the "gut" of the slope. Soon, she was heading down past the cliff, straight for the gaping bergschrund.

Bergschrunds have a nasty habit of swallowing people. Often, a thin layer of snow is all that covers the gaping crevasse, so when skiers or climbers fall inside, they end up getting trapped underneath the glacier. "The one on Mendenhall Towers the year I did it was about three metres wide and really scary," Victoria remembers. "Noah broke his arm jumping over it."

Victoria cruised towards the bergschrund, knowing she would need a lot of speed to safely clear the three-metre gap. She also knew from talking to the other riders that the landing was super sketchy and probably almost as dangerous as the gap itself. Still, she had no choice; she had to jump. She flew into the air and crashed down onto the chunky, icy snow on the other side. It was a spectacular crash to end a spectacular run, but thankfully Victoria wasn't injured, just a little bruised. Mendenhall was done, and Victoria had cemented her place among the best big-mountain riders in the world. Clearly, this girl wasn't just along for the ride.

Riding into the Future

A decade has passed since the Standard Films release documenting the first snowboard descent of Mendenhall Towers came out, and things have changed a lot in Alaska. For one thing, it's a lot safer than it used to be—the riders are required to bring an experienced guide along with them whenever they fly into the mountains. Victoria, for one, likes it better that way.

"We still usually pick our own terrain," she says, "but the guide is there to assess the snow pack and the situation, and to help us in the event of an emergency. If we're going to set up to do something, they're going to set themselves up in order to deal with stuff if something goes wrong."

There are still endless opportunities for exploration in Alaska; hundreds of peaks that Victoria has yet to even lay eyes on, let alone to carve some turns down their powdery faces and steep couloirs. As well, in the areas where Victoria has already ridden, things change every year. "Maybe there's something that always looked undoable, but now suddenly there's snow stuck to that rock, so it creates a line that never existed before."

"It's going to be a while before most peaks are ridden," she says. "And the thing is, it's hard for anyone to keep track of what's been ridden and what hasn't. I don't know if anyone really knows. Lots of people think they're doing first descents, and they don't know that people did it way back when, but never told anyone."

There's a good chance it *was* ridden way back when. After all, it's been 10 or 12 years since Victoria Jealouse and her crazy friends were flying to peaks seemingly at random and carving more first descents than they could count down snow faces in the middle of the Alaskan wilderness.

CHAPTER THREE

Etienne Gilbert:
Battle to the Top

That Elusive Winning Feeling

ETIENNE GILBERT WOKE TO THE SOUND OF LAUGHING nearby. Who was laughing? Where was he? He opened his eyes and realized where he'd fallen asleep. He was lying on a bench under a big tent

Etienne Gilbert floats a huge method air at Brohm Ridge.

beside the snowboard park on Vancouver's Mount Seymour. He'd competed that morning in the qualifying round of the Boardroom Slopestyle Contest. He had qualified. He fell back to sleep with a smile on his face.

An hour or so later, he woke up again. Where was everybody? Where were his friends? *Where was his board?* Etienne looked around. There it was, leaning up against a nearby table. He grabbed it and headed up to the lift to work out his sore muscles with a few practice runs through the park. It was a good park, good for his style of riding. It had nice hits and good rails. He tried to figure out a run, but his head wasn't in it.

Why hadn't he slept the night before? The answer was simple: the day before nobody had thought the Boardroom's annual slopestyle competition was going to happen. The contest had already been put off for a day because of bad weather, and everyone had expected the same thing to happen again. Fog and rain had plagued the mountain for days. In a slopestyle contest, the riders have to complete a run down through a park, hitting obstacles and performing tricks all the way down. Visibility is key. The competitors need to be able to see what's coming up. The bad weather didn't seem like it was going to lift, so Etienne and his friends had done what any Whistlerites would do if they were stuck in the city: they went out and partied their faces off until the wee hours of morning.

The next day, the weather cleared somewhat, and the contest was on. Etienne and his friends woke just in time to make it to the hill for the qualifying session. Etienne felt some of the familiar excitement riding in a competition gave him, but he doubted he was going to do well; he was just too tired. He had never won a big contest. It was high time he did. But it wouldn't be this contest. Not today.

From his seat on the chairlift, Etienne watched a competitor slip off the side of the huge box obstacle in the middle of the course and land on his butt in the snow. *At least I have the box dialled in*, Etienne thought to himself. Everyone else was struggling like mad with that thing. "That's going to be the difference," he said to himself.

It was Etienne's turn to run the course for the judges. "Next up, from Québec, it's Etienne Gilbert!" said the announcer over the music coming from the loudspeakers. The crowd lining the run cheered as Etienne waved half-heartedly from the start line. What should he do first? *Focus, you've got to focus*, he told himself before launching down the run.

He started with an air-to-fakie off the first jump and landed solidly on his feet. That set him up for his next jump, a cab 540.

If I can actually land these two first jumps, he told himself, *I'll take it from there.*

He flew off the lip with a smoothness honed by years of practice and smacked down on the sloped landing on the far side of the jump.

He had landed on his feet again. He couldn't believe it.

The crowd was screaming like mad. Suddenly he was focused. Suddenly, there was something at stake. The world seemed to slow down around him, and all he could see was the giant plastic-covered wooden box jutting out of the snow in front of him.

It was 2001, and the rail and box-riding craze in snowboarding was gaining momentum. Many pro riders were still struggling to slide on rails and boxes with any style, but not Etienne. He'd caught on fast, and his rail tricks were gaining him a lot of attention. He knew that if he could land a good trick on this big box, it might be enough to set him apart from the other riders.

He launched off the snow, spinning himself 270° in the air before landing sideways on the slippery top sheet. He slid to the end of the box then jumped and spun himself another 270° before landing on the snow.

The crowd went nuts. They'd never seen anything like it. But the Etienne Gilbert show wasn't over yet. Etienne, now riding backwards, was heading down the slope towards the last obstacle, a long rail. He launched into the air, careful not to spin too hard, and landed with his board perfectly perpendicular on the rail. The base of his board slid smoothly along the rail before he executed a perfect dismount onto the snow. What a run!

A few more competitors wound through the park, but none of them could put anything comparable together. Etienne had finally won his first major contest, and the victory had come on a day when he could hardly keep his eyes open. He drove back to his adopted hometown of Whistler $5000 richer and a whole lot more confident. It may have been the first win for Etienne, but he knew it wouldn't be his last. Now that he'd figured out what he was capable of, there was no stopping him.

"You start believing" Etienne muses, when questioned about how he felt after that first competitive victory at Mount Seymour in 2001. "When you win one, you start thinking, 'Hey, I can do this,' you know? It's a big thing to know that it can actually happen, that you can have a good day."

Humble Beginnings

Etienne Gilbert was born on December 16, 1978, in the small town of St-Rédempteur, on the south shore of the St. Lawrence River, near Québec City. He grew up playing hockey, but at the age of 15, he quit and started snowboarding.

"I have always loved sports," he says. "They've always been my reason to live. When I gave snowboarding a try, I fell in love. Life soon became all about snowboarding. It's the one sport that allowed me to discipline myself the way I wanted and to go in the direction that I wished."

Almost every day after school, Etienne and his friends hiked down to the escarpments above the mighty St. Lawrence River to build jumps and learn the tricks they had seen on videos. When they could scam a ride, they headed up to the local hills to ride under the lights.

The winter after Etienne finished high school, the Mont-Sainte-Anne ski resort, not far from Québec City, decided to purchase a new piece of equipment, known as a pipe-dragon, to sculpt perfect half-pipes. Etienne began spending every day he could up at Sainte-Anne learning how to ride pipe.

Some of the pipe riders from Mont-Sainte-Anne were really pushing it at that time, guys like David Carrier-Porcheron and Etienne Tremblay. Etienne Gilbert was impressed by their riding and impressed by the fact that Québecers were making their mark on the snowboarding world. Etienne knew if he rode hard enough himself, he could become as good and consistent as them. He began riding every chance he got, determined to see how far he could go if he gave it his all.

Spring came, and while most Québecers got out their bikes and lawnmowers, Etienne stayed inside watching snowboard movies and studying the moves of the world's top pros. He was obsessed. Before long, he couldn't handle it anymore. If he stayed in Québec, he wouldn't be able to ride for months. How was he supposed to get better if he couldn't even ride? There was only one thing to do: ride the summer season on Whistler's Blackcomb

Glacier. No simple matter of geography was going to stop him now!

The Big Move

A few weeks later, Etienne was out west, firmly ensconced in his own version of the Whistler life. Around the time his friends were getting home from the bar, he was waking up and heading off to bake bagels. After that, he'd ride all afternoon, then head home early to sleep while his friends were out partying.

"All I wanted to do was snowboard; snowboard my brains out, and that's what I did. I didn't party at all," he remembers. "There were a lot of French guys out there that summer, and those guys were going off every night, drinking, partying, and I was being super quiet, trying to save money and riding every day."

The next fall, Etienne was supposed to return to Québec for school. That never happened. He had fallen in love with the snowboarding lifestyle. He got a season's pass through his job at the Beaver Tails Snack Stop and rode hard whenever he wasn't working.

Etienne entered every contest he could. Soon, he was getting noticed by the snowboarding community and even managed to pick up a few sponsors. Then in 2001, he picked up his first contest win at the Boardroom Slopestyle. He knew that wasn't enough, though; he needed a bigger break than that if he was going to make it in the impossibly competitive world of professional snowboarding.

That break would come but not before a reckless fall almost ended his career.

Superpark Madness

Every year, *Snowboarder* magazine hosts an event called Superpark where the jumps are massive and the crashes spectacular. Etienne headed down to the Superpark 4 session at Mammoth Mountain, California, in the spring of 2002, determined to bust large and take home some glory. But when he got there, he realized what he was up against. The park was insane; the jumps were huger than anything he'd ever seen.

Etienne stood at the top of the park, sizing up the hits. He'd been jumping these massive hits all day, but he still felt nervous. He just couldn't get used to them; they were too huge. The hip, protruding from the slope, like a massive mutant snow beast's spinal cord, was easily 30 metres long. You had to hit it straight on with a lot of speed and pick your side. People were going huge, but despite his jangled nerves, Etienne was determined to push it to the next level.

With no thought of the consequences, he motored down over the snow, determined to make his mark on Mammoth. He would make his mark, all right, but not in the way he had hoped. Instead of hitting the jump high, which would have put him on the right trajectory to land farther down the side of the spine than everybody else, he got caught up in the main track taken by all the other riders. The next thing he knew, he was flying straight off the jump and over the safety of the steep, sloped landing, flying towards a bone-crushing landing on the flat.

"I felt like I was dropping off a cliff to the flat!" Etienne says, remembering the dread he felt when he realized he was going to overshoot the landing. He crashed down hard on the unforgiving snow and literally bounced back into the air from the force of his landing. His Superpark session was done...and so was his season. Etienne found out later he had torn the anterior cruciate ligament (ACL) in his knee, which would require surgery before he could take to the hills again.

Etienne learned a lot that day. Mainly, he learned that he had to be careful not to get caught up in the moment and not to push himself too hard, especially when it didn't feel right. "You have to know your limits and when to push them," he said afterwards. "When I blew my knee, I was pushing too hard at the wrong time, for the wrong reason."

The Crown Prince of Québec

After his surgery, Etienne was chilling out in Québec, working at the snowboard shop and wondering what he was going to do with his life. He knew that if he was going to make it as a snowboarder, he would have to return to Whistler, but he wasn't looking forward to it.

He needed to buy a new snowmobile so he could go out into the Whistler backcountry with the filmmakers and photographers who would make him famous, but how was he supposed to afford that? The money he'd saved wouldn't even cover his first month's rent in Whistler. He was broke, looking forward to another wasted season riding the mountain and relying on his friends to get him into the backcountry. There was also his knee to worry about. Would he still want to go big and hit everything or be daunted by the fear that he might re-injure himself? Etienne was as determined as ever, but he could feel despair eating away at him. Then the phone call came.

It was his team manager from the clothing company Sessions, one of his sponsors. They wanted him to ride in the Vans Triple Crown in Breckenridge, Colorado.

"How's your knee? Can you compete?" the manager asked.

"I can compete," Etienne said. He wasn't 100 percent, but he couldn't miss this chance to get back in the game.

A few weeks later, Etienne was knocking on the door of the giant lodge Sessions had rented for the competition. A guy Etienne didn't recognize answered the door. Inside, people were sprawled everywhere. There was hardly room to sit down, let alone sleep. His sponsors had told Etienne he would have his own bed. *Oh well*, he thought. Sometimes you just had to roll with it.

The next day broke sunny and beautiful, and Etienne leaped up from where he had crashed out in his sleeping bag on the floor the night before. People were sleeping everywhere, and the lodge was trashed. The night before had been a bit of a party, but for Etienne, the real craziness would go down on the slopes. He bent his weaker leg a few times, flexing his knee. "Feels good," he muttered to himself. "Let's do this."

A few hours later, Etienne was standing at the top of the slope, waiting to take a practice run through the park. The Vans Triple Crown Slopestyle event was like the one at Mount Seymour but longer— a mix of jumps and rails stretching down two sides of a giant park. One side was bigger than the other. Etienne was sticking to the smaller side; he preferred its flow.

"I feel like absolute hell," a hungover-looking competitor said as he pulled up beside him. Etienne smiled but said nothing. The rider dropped in and bombed full speed towards the first huge jump on the left side of the park.

"Idiot," said Etienne, shaking his head and remembering his own crash at Mammoth the previous season. The unidentified rider flew off balance into the air, his arms waving wildly as he tried to keep his board underneath his body. It was no use. He came crashing down on his butt on the far side of the jump and lay still. Two ski patrollers skied down and closed the jump.

Etienne was a little shaken after seeing the fall, but he felt good. His practice runs were going well; he couldn't remember ever feeling so confident, so ready at a competition. He'd found his rhythm, and he was ready to throw down.

Finally it was time. "Alright, dudes," said the official at the top of the run. "You've got two runs to make it count. The judges will only count the best run. ARE YOU READY?"

"YEAH!" shouted the riders. Etienne stayed quiet. He was staring down at the run below him. He knew exactly what he wanted to do this time, and he knew he could do it. "I'm so ready, you have no idea," he muttered to himself.

"Etienne GILL-BURT" said the official, mispronouncing his name, just like his friends in Whistler always did.

"I'm here," he said, popping to his feet and sliding down to the starting gate.

"Whenever you're ready," the official said. Etienne took a few deep breaths to steady himself. Seconds later, his mind was clear. He turned and jumped into the air, landing with a fair amount of speed on the in-ramp.

The first obstacle, a box that was flat for half its length and then sloped downwards, got closer and closer. With the confidence of a quarterback who knows he's already sunk the other team, Etienne leaped into the air, spinning wildly. He spun almost a full turn before landing, still spinning, on the box. He slid and spun another turn on *top* of the box and then, still spinning madly, dismounted onto the snow.

The crowd went insane.

"Oh yeah? You wanna see something?" Etienne muttered under his breath, challenging the unseen opponent who had occupied his mind since the first day he'd strapped on a snowboard. He flew up the first jump and launched into the stratosphere, spinning to the left and grabbing his board with all his strength. Around and around he went, two full rotations, before gracefully coming down on the landing. This show was ON!

The crowd was now going ballistic. Who was this Canadian Maniac?

Etienne attacked the next jump, spinning hard to the right one and a half times, like a monkey play-fully thrown out of its favourite tree. *Too big. TOO BIG*, Etienne thought to himself. He was going huge. Could he possible stick this jump? BANG! He rode away with nary a knuckle dragging on the snow.

I'm on it, no question. There was still one jump and two rails left. He bombed backwards towards the last jump and then launched himself into his next trick, spinning the hard way with enough momentum to bring him around one and a half times so that he landed facing forward. A perfect switch backside 540. Two rails later, he was finished.

In the end, it was the run of the day, and Etienne Gilbert suddenly found himself with $12,000 US in his pocket. It was enough money to buy a sled *and* a new truck! The win also meant he was invited to the X-Games, the biggest snowboarding event in the world, other than perhaps the Olympics.

"I was so pumped," he says, remembering that amazing day. "My sponsors were happy; I was going to the X-Games; and I had some money so I could go back to Whistler."

Suddenly, the future looked a whole lot brighter.

Etienne Gilbert slashes a wind lip. Who says this kid can't ride powder?

The Riding Life

Etienne went back to Whistler, bought a sled and a truck and started working on some of the gnarliest snowboard video parts coming out of Canada at the time. As he soon found out, though, not every day in the backcountry around Whistler is gravy. Often, it's a lot of work with little reward.

"Some days you get up there, and you don't really find anything to do because either the snow is bad or it's cloudy, and you're like 'I can't believe we came all the way here and we didn't do anything'," he says. "You're like, 'I didn't get a sled to come up here and ride around; I want to snowboard!'"

Also, the backcountry around Whistler gets more crowded year after year. More snowboarders, more skiers, more snowmobilers and a lot more film crews and photographers head out for the powder every good day of the winter.

"It's often a race," Etienne explains. "It can get pretty funny when you're racing your friends from the parking lot because you know they might want to go to the same place as you do, but they're with a different film crew."

Finding a unique spot to film is getting harder and harder, but Etienne remembers one day when he went up with his friend, photographer Colin Adair from *Snowboard Canada*, and they found what they were looking for. "We found a couple of cool features, and I ended up getting an interview and a few photos in the magazine out of it."

One of the two sequences Colin Adair took that day shows Etienne nonchalantly rolling backwards off a giant, puffy cornice drop that would strike fear into most weekend warriors. Once in the air, he does a backwards somersault while spinning one and a half times to land facing forwards. The other sequence shows Etienne spinning a 360 off a huge jump, smacking the top of a tree with his board mid-spin and landing perfectly far down the slope in the powder. The sun's out, the snow is glistening and the mountains in the distance look spectacular. What you don't see in the pictures is all the hard work behind the photos.

"The good days are worth all the bad days you can have," Etienne says. "There's always something funny happening, and as long as you have a good crew and people are positive and motivated, and not bitchy, then you'll have fun. If you get too caught up in this job, you lose the whole point."

Shake it Down

Ever since its inception in 2002, Etienne had been going back to Québec for the annual Empire Shakedown competition at Mont St.-Sauveur. The contest run consists of one giant jump followed by a set of stairs with a rail going down the middle and ledges on either side. To win, the rider must cleanly complete tricks on both the jump and the stairs.

The scene at Shakedown is total madness. Thousands of kids pack into the base area around the bottom of the course, music blares out of the speakers, loads of free stuff is tossed into the crowd, and every time a rider lands something good, the crowd goes nuts. The energy is infectious, and the riders respond to it. Etienne counts the Empire Shakedown as his favourite contest. It's in his home province, and he loves the atmosphere. In the spring of 2004, he headed out to Québec ready to win. Unfortunately, so did a lot of the best riders in the world; guys like Mike Page, T.J. Schneider, Mikey Rencz and the previous year's winner, Guillaume Brochu.

Etienne narrowly qualified for the finals scheduled to take place under the lights after the sun went down. When the finals got underway, the crowd was bigger and rowdier than ever before at the contest. People were going nuts, and a giant fight broke out after someone threw a snowboard into the crowd. Once the chaos had died down, it was time for everyone to focus their attention on the riding, as some of the sickest jumpers in the history of the sport hucked for glory.

The riders were pulling out all the stops, and Etienne knew that if he wanted to win that night, he was going to have to do likewise. He had started trying for a full three rotations off the jump (a frontside 1080) earlier that day, but he hadn't landed it. The clock was ticking, and Etienne figured he had time for at least one more practice jump. He would practice the 1080 again; it was his only chance.

Etienne launched himself down the steep run, keeping his legs bent and winding up his shoulders. This was going to take some spin! He launched into the air off the colossal jump and over the flat area; cameramen were milling about far below him. He was spinning wildly. Would he get all the way around? He didn't even know where the landing was. Finally, he came around enough to spot the landing far below him.

He landed on his feet, but his board was perpendicular to the slope and he slid out onto his butt. "Pretty close," he said to himself, but was it close enough to risk everything and try the 1080 during his judged run?

Etienne trudged back up the snowy slope to the top of the run. He was tired, and he was losing his focus. He got to the top of the run and sat down at a picnic table to catch his breath. The crowd in the riders' tent was thinning out; most riders had already completed their two judged runs. Time was ticking by, and Etienne sat there, still not sure what to do. Fifteen minutes passed. Finally, he roused himself. "What am I doing," he said quietly. "I can't sit here all night."

A few riders were still practicing. "What a run!" shouted the announcer over the loudspeakers after one rider completed the course. "Was that judged? No? No, it wasn't judged. What a shame. That might have been the run of the night!"

What if that happened to Etienne? He couldn't handle this. He sighed and looked up to where T. J. Schneider was getting ready to go.

"It's T.J. Schneider. He's dropping in for his final judged run," said the announcer. "He's going for a frontside 1080!" Etienne's heart sank. That was his trick! *If he lands this, I'm done*, he thought. T.J. spun off the jump and grabbed his board. It looked good until he disappeared from sight over the lip of the landing. Etienne waited to hear from the announcer if he'd landed it. "OOOHHHHH!" A big groan emanated from the crowd at the bottom of the hill. "So close," said the announcer.

Etienne jumped to his feet. He had to go now; before someone landed a good, judged run and claimed the contest.

"Frontside 1080, and a frontside boardslide on the rail," he told the official holding the radio. The official relayed the information to the judges at the bottom of the hill.

Etienne dropped in. He rocketed towards the jump. "Let's DO THIS!" he said to himself, seconds before firing into the sky far above the St.-Sauveur resort. The world was off-kilter, blurry and confusing. Up and down had ceased to make sense. So had left and right. Etienne grasped his board by the toe edge with his leading hand, trying to keep himself compact so he would spin faster. Suddenly, the whirling chaos around him began to slow down and come into focus, and he spotted the landing between his feet.

BAM! He came down perfectly centred on the landing. *I'm standing*, he thought. *NO WAY!* He could hear the crowd screaming support for one of their own, a Québecer. Now he just had to land the rail. Etienne fixed his goggles and rocketed over the flat spot between the landing of the jump and the stairs. He'd only landed the frontside boardslide on the down-flat-down rail once so far that day. It was a crazy trick, and he was one of only a few that had tried it. Now, if he wanted the $10,000, he had to land it. He'd told the judges that he was going to do it; there was no backing out now.

I've got too much speed, he thought, just as his board left the snow. It was too late to slow down now! He jammed his board down on the rail, his butt facing the landing and his shoulders twisted to keep him centred for the slide. He slid down the first part of the rail, onto the flat part and then down the last sloping part, before plopping his board down into the spring corn snow below. His hands shot up in the air in a premature victory celebration. The crowd went wild and a few enthusiastic souls even jumped the fence to hug their new hero. He knew he had won for sure this time!

"I felt a little lucky," says Etienne, remembering his victory at the Empire Shakedown. "But at the same time, I felt like I gave it my best shot, and I earned it. The other riders kind of convinced me that I was a threat. So I was like, alright then, I'll win it."

Years of practice and commitment to his sport had allowed Etienne Gilbert to perfect his snowboarding and become one of the best riders in the world. And once he found his confidence, he began to claim his rightful spot on the podium.

CHAPTER FOUR

Justin Lamoureux: Pipe Dreams

Half-Pipe Hero in the Making

"AS MUCH AS I CAN, I'M OUT IN THE BACKCOUNTRY," SAYS Canadian half-pipe team rider Justin Lamoureux. "It's my favourite thing to do on a snowboard— just go out and ride with a few buddies. Ride the powder, cruise around, hit whatever…"

Justin Lamoureux isn't afraid to spin a 360 off a huge back-country drop.

This may be true, but Justin's skills at playing around in the fluff, dropping cliffs in the middle of nowhere or slashing turns down first descents, like the one he made on Cascade Mountain near Banff with Kyle Wolochatiuk in 1999, aren't what have made him famous. Justin's skill in the half-pipe is what has brought him worldwide attention. His smooth, technical approach to destroying the U-jump is incredible to watch, even if it's not what he enjoys the most.

Over the years, he has made a name for himself as one of the most technical half-pipe riders this country has ever seen. Huge spins, massive switch airs, insane combos and the dedication, focus and determination to consistently place at the top of the field in World Cup half-pipe contests are what bring the back bacon into this Whistlerite's Canadian kitchen.

It all started in New Jersey where Justin was born. Soon after he learned to walk, he began surfing the waves of the Jersey coastline and skateboarding on his off days. Then, in 1988, Justin's family moved to Ottawa. Since there was no surfing in Ottawa, his parents decided to buy their hyperactive son a new toy to keep him busy—a snowboard. For Christmas, Justin got a 150-cm long Kemper Mini-Rampage. Riding sideways wasn't a new sensation to Justin, and after only two lessons, he was slashing his way down the runs under the lights at nearby Camp Fortune ski hill in the Gatineaus.

"My parents would drop me off from school and pick me up at 9 PM," he remembers. "I was going whenever I could. I was all about snowboarding as soon as I got it."

Justin's parents eventually moved to Toronto, deep in flattest Ontario. Luckily for Justin, they sent their son off to boarding school at Bishop's College School in Québec's Eastern Townships. Whenever he wasn't playing hockey with the school team, Justin was up riding at one of the many ski hills nearby.

Life was good, until Justin graduated from high school and went off to the University of Waterloo in Ontario to study engineering. He was stuck in the heartland of Ontario, far from the powdery slopes of Québec's Eastern Townships. He refused to give up, though, and whenever he had a chance, he jumped in the car with his brother Marty to drive down to Québec to ride Mount Orford.

The next year, things got even worse. Justin hardly got a chance to snowboard, and he was starting to question the direction his life was taking.

"I was stuck at school all winter," he remembers. "My friends and I would go up to Blue Mountain every now and then, but there were certain times when I couldn't go riding for like a month. I was going nuts!"

Finally, it was spring, and Justin could finally forget about snowboarding and focus on homework. He was in a co-op program that ran all through the year. It consisted of four months of work, followed by four months of school, followed by another four months of work. He was doing well. He was focused. Then he did something that would change everything: he decided to take a work term in Calgary. Worse still, he decided that before he started, he would take a little late-season trip to Lake Louise to go snowboarding for a month.

Before he could pull out his scientific calculator to compute the effects of a month of extreme riding on his engineering career, Justin was ripping down powder lines at the Lake with the likes of Jonovan Moore, Joey Mosberg, Gregg Todds, Trevor Flemming and Andrew Hardingham. The Banff guys had no mercy; they laid bare for Justin all the natural wonders of the Lake and exposed the poor eastern transplant to the best snowboarding of his life.

"I remember Jonovan. He was just like, 'Let's go do it!'" Justin remembers, laughing. "The first run I took with him, he did this huge backside 360 off a cornice, and I was just like, 'Whoa! Game on!'"

Then it was time to go back to work.

Justin spent that summer working in Calgary, but practically every weekend, he was up in Banff visiting his new friends and laying the groundwork for a life in the mountains, far from any engineering labs. It was almost a foregone conclusion that Justin would decide not to return to school the following winter. Instead he packed his bags and moved to Banff for four months to try and survive on a diet of powder turns and Chinese noodles.

That winter, Justin's riding improved rapidly. By the end of the season, after entering several local Alberta contests, he felt ready to compete against the rest of Canada. Justin and some of his friends went to the half-pipe Nationals in Ontario, where he finished in 10th place. The more Justin rode, the better he got, and the more he wanted to do it.

"I knew beforehand that I could compete, and that proved it. I figured that all these guys are riding the whole time, and I'm doing stuff that they can do even though I'm only riding a month out of the year and going to school."

Still, if Justin was going to pursue snowboarding, something had to change. He decided to try to work something out with his school. After much begging and pleading, he was able to arrange his schedule so that he could study for four months, work for four months and take four months off every winter to snowboard. How did he do it? It was simple: he told everyone he wanted to go the Olympics. Well, say something enough times and you start to believe it.

A Personal Victory

The arrangement Justin had made with his school worked out well for a few seasons. Justin began to enter bigger contests. He was riding hard and trying his best to compete against top-level riders in the half-pipe. In 1998, he headed down to the US Open in Stratton, Vermont, for the second time, to see how he measured up against the likes of Terje Haakonsen, Daniel Franck, Todd Richards and Canadian phenom Mike Michalchuk.

The contest, hailed as the premiere event in snowboarding, attracted thousands of spectators that year. People were literally hanging out of the trees. Justin was so psyched to be taking part in this historic contest—the brainchild of Jake Burton, the accepted godfather of snowboarding—but that didn't affect his focus. As always, Justin was there to compete.

The day of the event dawned overcast and misty, but the contest was on. Unlike the majority of the competitors that year, Justin had managed to get a good night's sleep, eat a healthy breakfast and fit in a solid stretching session that morning. He was as ready as he'd ever been to throw down some runs in the pipe.

The scene that day was absolute chaos. People lined the top of each side of the half-pipe three deep, straining their necks to get a good look as the riders flew high overhead on their way down the pipe. Michalchuk was practising double back flips. It looked like he was going six metres out of the pipe! People in the crowd were freaking out, and the riders were feeding off their energy. Everyone was totally stoked. Justin was practically running up the half-pipe after every run, and his tireless energy paid off. Before he knew it, he had made it through the qualifying session and was riding in the semi-finals.

The top 16 would make it to the finals. *Top 16*, Justin thought to himself. There were probably 100 guys there he had heard of. How was he going to beat any of them? He just had to stay focused and keep it light. Keep having fun. Without a doubt, he was having a great time, riding better than he ever had in a contest, taking big risks and pushing his airs as high as he could out of the pipe.

Finally, it was time for his run. Without hesitating, he dropped in and launched what felt like the biggest backside air of his life. The crowd went nuts. He landed squarely back on the wall, pumped down it for speed and flew across the flat bottom and up the opposite wall. As he launched into the air, he grabbed his board and began to spin upside down. With his knees tucked into his chest and his body compact, it looked like he was in control, but had he gone too high? It was the biggest he had ever gone in a contest. Would he be able to stick the landing? Still spinning, Justin rocketed back towards the snowy lip of the pipe. Then, just as it looked like disaster was imminent, his feet were underneath him, and he finessed his board down onto the sloped transition.

The crowd went ballistic, urging him on.

He had hardly lost any speed on the landing, which was lucky, because he still had three more jumps. Three more good jumps, that was all he needed, and he would be in the finals. He pumped up the opposite wall and launched into the air again.

Another spin and another grab, but this time he had to land backwards. His board came around, and just in time, he spotted his landing beneath him. Wham! His board came down flat on the wall. It took all Justin's strength to stay on his feet as he looked over his shoulder at the opposite wall.

A split second later, he rocketed back into the air, this time spinning himself a full 720° to land facing forward down the ramp for his last jump. He had to go big. He pumped for speed and leaped into the air, but his speed was lagging and he didn't go as high as he'd hoped. Still, the crowd was cheering loudly, and he knew he'd had a solid run. Qualifying for the finals at the US Open would mean that Justin Lamoureux had finally arrived on the world stage. But could it possibly happen? He'd had a good run, but would it be enough?

Finally, the semi-finals were over, and the judges were gathered together working out the results. "Before we announce the finalists, we have an announcement to make," said one of the officials over the loudspeakers. "Due to adverse weather conditions during some of the runs, we've decided to let in the top 21 riders."

It's true that it had been fairly foggy all day, but it still seemed strange to Justin that the judges had decided to change the format for the finals as a result of the weather. They announced the top ten. Justin's name was not among them. They got to number 15 and still no Justin. Then...

"Sixteenth, Justin Lamoureux from Canada!" said the announcer. Justin couldn't believe it. He'd qualified! They went on to read all the names including the two riders who had tied for 20th place. One of them was Burton rider Terje Haakonsen. Suddenly, it all made sense. Terje was arguably the best freestyle snowboarder in the world at that time. They couldn't hold the US Open final without Terje in it.

"Daniel Franck was in 19th place, and Terje was in 20th, and I was this kid in 16th," Justin remembers. "They read out those names, and I was like, 'Are you kidding me?' I couldn't believe that I'd actually gotten in ahead of these guys. I actually made the finals, and then Jake Burton had to pull the plug to get Terje in there. I didn't care though, because I legitimately made it into the finals."

In the end, Terje got second place behind Rob Kingwill, and Justin got 18th. He went home more certain than ever that he wasn't just a weekend warrior, an engineer pretending to be a snowboarder. He was a contender.

Olympic Dreams

The previous summer, Justin had wrangled a work term in Vancouver so he could be close enough to Whistler to get in some summer riding on the glacier. In July, he got a letter in the mail saying he had been accepted to take part in the national team try-outs camp. He went to work and asked his new boss for a week off so he could take part in the camp. The boss was less than understanding.

"You're either a professional engineer, or you do the other things in your life," he told Justin. It was the wrong thing to say. The following morning, Justin was on the bus bound for a friend's couch in Whistler, his future as an engineer in a holding pattern once again.

The camp was a relaxed and friendly affair, but Justin gave it all he had, knowing he was going to have to explain to his parents why he had once again let school slide in favour of snowboarding.

A week later, he was back on the bus down to Vancouver to get the rest of his stuff. In his hands, he clutched his letter of acceptance onto the Canadian national team. The gamble had paid off. Now it was going to be a whole lot easier for him to explain himself. He was serious about snowboarding because he was good at it. The next winter he might even end up at the Olympics, and to even have a shot at that was enough reason to drop everything, even a very promising career as an engineer. All that could wait. Right now, it was snowboarding.

Nevertheless, that fall, after a long summer of riding the Blackcomb Glacier, Justin returned to school in Waterloo. He excelled as usual in his classes, but as the time for the Olympic trials loomed closer, he grew more and more anxious. He was fit, but would he be able to ride well enough to make the team after several months off the snow?

December finally rolled around. Justin handed in his last exam and boarded a plane for Calgary. The try-outs were held at the Olympic Park. Justin gave it his all, but his double life as an academic meant he was stepping on his board for the first time that season. Everyone else was warmed up and ready to ride. He pulled out all the stops, but it wasn't enough. Justin would not join the Canadian team in Nagano. He would have to wait four more years before he could try again for the Salt Lake City Olympics in 2002.

During those four years, Justin wrapped up his studies, moved to Whistler and started riding like mad. Finally, he could focus on his passion. He entered every contest he could and placed consistently at the top of the field. In 1999, and again in 2001, he won the Canadian half-pipe Nationals, but with the Salt Lake City Olympics rapidly approaching, he couldn't crack the top 10 in any World Cup Competitions. Injuries plagued him throughout the 2001 season, and the best finish he could pull of that year in World Cup competition was 14th. It wasn't enough. Under the new rules for Canada's team selection, Justin did not make the cut for Salt Lake City.

After two heart-breaking attempts to make the Olympic team, Justin's resolve just grew stronger. The Olympic dream that was once an excuse to get his teachers to let him leave school early was now consuming him. When the 2004-05 season got underway—the season that would decide who would represent Canada at the Torino Winter Olympics— Justin exploded onto the competitive scene.

In December, he travelled down to Breckenridge, Colorado, for a Nor-Am Cup event to practice his run for the World Championships scheduled to take place in Whistler the following month. The judges loved the run and awarded Justin a bronze medal at the competition.

Buoyed by his good showing at Breckenridge, Justin drove north, knowing a good finish at the World Championships in Whistler would as good as guarantee him a spot on the Olympic team.

A Cloudy Day with a Silver Lining

As is all too typical in Whistler during the early season, it was raining and foggy the day of the contest. Nevertheless, the atmosphere surrounding the pipe on the lower slopes of Blackcomb was one of feverish anticipation. Both the contestants and the audience were well aware of the significance of the World Championships one season before an Olympics. Riders were sailing as high out of the soggy pipe as they could and taking some spectacular crashes.

Justin was riding as hard as any of them, practising the run he'd perfected in Breckenridge. Every pipe is different, and Justin knew if he hardwired the imperfections of this one into his brain, there was less chance he would spill. Finally, it was time for qualifying, and Justin pulled out the run. It went down like a warm drink on a cold Whistler evening with the judges, and they qualified him in third place.

Justin headed home to rest for a few hours before the evening finals under the lights. As he sat in his living room with his friends playing some video games, he reflected on his snowboarding career up to that point. It was a career, after all. It may have started out as a love affair, but now it was his life. His sponsors paid the bills, and he travelled the world riding his snowboard. There was no longer room for anything else. Snowboarding had brought him this far, but how much further could it take him? He passed his controller to a friend and walked into the kitchen to make some dinner.

He had just over an hour to eat and stretch. Then it would be time to head up the mountain. He was ready. He would show the hometown crowd, his friends, his family, his sponsors, all the other competitors and finally himself, that the years of dedication and hard work had been worth it. He hadn't been embarking on an empty dream. He had what it takes, and that night he was going to prove it.

Two hours later, Justin stood with the Canadian team's tuning technician, J.P. Trottier, at the top of the pipe. "I need to go faster, J.P. I don't care how much wax you have to put on my board, I have to go bigger."

J.P. scraped another layer of wax into the base of Justin's board. "Voila. That should do fine," he said as Justin reached for his board. "Ah, ah, ah, mon ami. Un petit moment," J.P. reached for a glass of water sitting in the snow beside him. "Regarde bien ca," he said.

He poured the water onto the upturned base of Justin's board. Even though the board was lying totally flat on the tuning bench, the water beaded, scurried off the edges and dripped down onto the snow. "C'est hallucinant, non?" J.P. said smiling and shaking his head.

"Yeah, cool," Justin said. "Can I have my board back now? I have a contest to win."

Justin had time for one more practice run through the pipe before the contest got underway. The run went well, and Justin knew, thanks to J.P., he had the fastest board out there.

For the finals, the riders had two runs to show their stuff to the judges. The judges would count only the best run of the two. The second run's order depended on how well the rider did during the first run. Ten riders were in the finals; Justin was eighth.

He dropped in for his first run.

Switch.

It was unheard of.

Very rarely will riders drop in for a half-pipe run backwards because their first jump is their most important. They need to go as big as they can in order to keep their speed for the rest of the run. Still, Justin was determined *not* to play by the usual rules. He needed to stand out.

He launched off the first wall and soared into the air, grabbing his board by the heel edge.

"That's switch, folks!" said the announcer over the loudspeakers. The massive crowd lining the tops of the half-pipe cheered as Justin brought his board back underneath him for the landing. It was easily the biggest switch backside air he'd ever done in a contest.

For once, technical wizard Justin Lamoureux keeps it simple. Yeah, right! Switch straight air into the void.

He rocketed towards the opposite wall. Bending his knees just at the right moment, he sprung into the air again. This time he spun while flipping his body upside down and grabbing his board by the toe edge—a move called a Haakonflip, after its inventor, Norwegian superstar Terje Haakonsen. Justin pulled it off with ease.

The next jump, a 900° spin while grabbing the tail of his board, was a tough one, but his board was going fast and Justin had turned his mind off before he even dropped in. He was going on autopilot, trusting his experience and training to get him through the difficult list of tricks. He flew into the air, spinning wildly. Would he make it around early enough to land smoothly and not lose any speed? Suddenly, there was the landing. Justin sucked up his knees and absorbed it. Two more tricks to go: a McTwist and a frontside 720. He'd done both tricks a million times before, so he pumped across the flat bottom trying to gather as much speed as he could before throwing himself as high into the air as possible. Both spins came down clean, and Justin pulled up at the bottom of the pipe as the crowd went mad for one of their own.

His second run didn't go nearly as well, but Justin knew that with his first run, he had a good chance of a podium finish. Now all he had to do was wait and see what the rest of the riders had up their sleeves.

Finnish superstar Antti Autti pulled off a sick run, just enough to knock Justin off the top spot, but at the end of the night Justin found himself climbing the podium to receive his first ever silver medal at a World Championships. His dream of global domination was now becoming a reality.

Torino in 2006

Later that same season, Justin finished fourth at a World Cup event in Lake Placid, New York. Then, just as things were beginning to look certain for the Olympics in 2006, Justin ventured into the powder-choked woods on Whistler with some friends, crashed into a tree and broke his leg.

It was a major bump in Justin's road to the Olympics, but the 29-year-old was determined not to let it get in the way of his dream. He spent the summer trying to stay fit and nursing his leg back into shape so he would be ready for the biggest competition of them all. If all goes as planned, he'll be ready to ride, and in a couple of months, he'll climb on a plane bound to Italy. He's got his whole run planned out already. It's going to be sick.

CHAPTER FIVE

Martin Gallant: Going Pro

"I'M GOING TO ENTER YOU IN THE PRO CATEGORY," SIMON Davis said to his friend Martin Gallant, grinning mischievously.

"No way," said Martin, shaking his head.

"Come on Martin, you're good. You can go down there and win that thing," Simon said picking up the phone.

Martin Gallant can destroy any kind of terrain, including huge backcountry booters like this one.

"I don't know Simon."

But Simon was already dialling. After talking for a while, Simon hung up and turned to face his friend, his grin growing wider. "You're in," he said.

Martin shook his head. "If you weren't injured, I swear I'd punch you," he said laughing.

Martin Gallant arrived in Whistler in the early days of snowboarding's exponential growth. He'd driven out from Québec in order to place himself closer to the centre of the Canadian snowboarding world. He'd already won dozens of races and half-pipe contests all across Canada, but he still hadn't earned any money as a snowboarder. It was time to start gambling, but he wasn't sure the Legendary Baker Banked Slalom race was a good place to start.

Still, a wild man with a reputation for getting crazy on and off the slope, Martin was pretty much up for anything. Which is ultimately why he found himself rocketing down the Sea-to-Sky highway in a Toyota van towards Mount Baker, in Washington State, for the Legendary Banked Slalom Race. At the wheel of the van was a new snowboarding friend Martin had met just days before—20-year-old Ross Rebagliati.

On the way to Baker, the two riders chatted about recent half-pipe contests and snowboard races they had entered. Soon the conversation turned to the Legendary Baker Banked Slalom, the race they were to compete in the next day.

"I heard Terje's gonna be there, and Sean Palmer," Martin said.

"I'm ready," Ross said, his eyes focused on the road ahead.

"We're gonna get killed," Martin said smiling. Whatever happened though, he didn't care. The young Québecer was having the time of his life. Every day was a new adventure. By that time, Martin had already been crowned Canadian half-pipe champion, and several years before, he had briefly reigned as Canada's slalom champion in his age category. His favourite event though, was moguls. Martin ruled the moguls, an event that no longer exists in snowboarding. Basically, Martin ruled everything. He was an all-around destroyer with a serious competitive streak. The field at the Legendary Banked Slalom that year may have intimidated him, but he was always ready to race.

The Banked Slalom race at Mount Baker is almost as old as the sport itself. Bob Barci, a local bike shop owner, and Tom Sims, owner and founder of Sims Snowboards, brought their idea of a banked slalom race to Mt. Baker because at the time, it was one of the few ski areas in North America that welcomed snowboarders. Plus, it had a natural half-pipe.

That first year, the race ran down the 600-metre natural gully on the White Salmon run. It was called the Sims Open, and the challenge was to beat organizer Tom Sims. The race took place on Super Bowl Sunday because the mountain's owner was afraid it would generate complaints from skiers. Twenty-eight pioneering riders, their primitive equipment held together with duct tape, steered their swallow-tailed boards up the banks of the gully and around the gates. In the end, Tom Sims was the winner with the fastest time.

Over the years, the course got longer and more challenging. By 1992, when Martin and Ross drove down from Whistler to compete in the race, it was a gruelling, thigh-burning course stretching almost the whole way down the hill. In later years, the race stopped handing out cash prizes to the winners of the pro categories, but in 1992, there was cash up for grabs; lots of it.

The morning of the race, Ross and Martin pulled into the crowded parking lot at Mount Baker, and they could feel the excitement in the air. Martin got out of the van and got his boot bag out of the back. He went back to the passenger side door, put his loose-fitting snowboarding pants on and laced up his soft boots. He was ready.

He shouted over to Ross who was on the other side of the van.

"I'll be ready in a minute," Ross said. After another minute or so, Martin went around the van to see what his new friend was doing. Ross was kneeling down buckling up a pair of hard racing boots. He was wearing a stretchy ski racing suit and a helmet.

"You're wearing all that stuff?" Martin asked, laughing. He looked around to see if anyone else had noticed Ross' ridiculous attire.

"Yup," Ross said, nodding.

"It's not that kind of race, man." Martin said.

Ross just smiled and slipped his goggles over his helmet.

Martin looked around again, embarrassed for his friend.

As Martin remembers it, during the early days of snowboarding it was definitely not cool to get caught trying too hard.

"Back then, if you were working too hard for it, you were a poser," he recalls laughing. "People didn't respect you. Snowboarding was hardcore. Snowboarding was from the top of the mountain to the bottom, no messing around."

In spite of snowboarding's dominant punk ethos at the time, Ross had his own ideas about going from the top of the mountain to the bottom. He didn't care about being cool, about fitting in with all the other more laid-back racers. He was there for one reason—to win. Martin admits that he was also super competitive back then; he was just better at hiding it.

Both Martin and Ross made it through to the finals. By his final run, Martin wasn't sure if he had any gas left in the tank, but before he knew what was going on, he was in the starting box waiting for the signal.

"Whenever you're ready, Martin," the official said. The French-Canadian ripper lunged up and over the starting gate, and his board shot down the run. Up and around he went. Up and around, up and around. He was going fast, he could tell. He just had to stay on course. At about the halfway point, his thighs began to burn from the effort of turning on the steep banks. "Keep going," Martin told himself. Up and around, up and around.

He felt like he was going to die. Was this thing ever going to end?

Finally, Martin came around the last turn and saw the finish line. He pointed his board towards it and tucked his hands in by his sides. He could feel the wind billowing the shell of his jacket behind him. *Too bad I don't have Ross' suit*, he thought to himself, smiling inwardly. He shot across the finish line, and the few spectators gathered around cheered for him as he flopped onto the snow, feeling as though he was going to be sick.

"Martin Gallant from Québec, Canada," the announcer said.

He had done well, Martin figured, considering it was his first time ever at the race. He decided to hang around and watch his friend Ross run through the last gates. A few minutes later, he saw Ross' slim profile careening down the mountain, his race board making short work of the gates.

"YEAH, ROSS!" Martin shouted. "GO FOR IT!"

Ross' pace didn't let up. He looked determined to win. He pounded through the last few gates and shot over the finish line, his eyes already looking up at the leader board. The number one went up by his name, and his hands shot up in the air.

"YEAH, ROSS!" Martin shouted again, running over to congratulate him.

In the end, Ross' time won out over the rest of the field, and he emerged as the winner of the 8th annual Legendary Banked Slalom. Martin Gallant finished in 6th place, which in those days meant he was eligible for a $2000 prize.

When Martin went up to get his prize, the officials explained that if he accepted the prize, it meant he was "going pro" and could no longer enter any amateur contests. "That was how it worked back

Huge gaps aren't a problem for Martin Gallant.

then," he explains. "You weren't a pro until you won a contest and accepted the money. I told them, 'Give me the money!' I didn't care; I needed it."

The prize money was great, the race was fun, but the best part of the weekend was yet to come. Some of the locals offered to show the Canadians a few of the local powder stashes. In fact, the proximity of Mount Baker's deep powder runs to the racecourse is one of the reasons many of the world's top snowboarders still make the trek to the small northwestern resort for the race. The organizers no longer award cash prizes, but you can't put a price on a friendly atmosphere and the chance to take part in one of the oldest and most prestigious snowboarding events on the calendar.

Martin hasn't been back to the Mount Baker's Legendary Banked Slalom since 1992. Instead, he has made a name for himself as one of Canada's best all-around snowboarders, slaying lines down some of the craziest peaks in Alaska and pushing the limits of the sport on the jumps. He can't explain why he's never made the short drive back down to Baker for the race, but he says there's always the possibility that he might once again give it a try.

As for Ross, he's been back since, but 1992 was the one and only year he won the famed event. Of course, in 1998, Ross had another, far more significant victory at the Olympics in Nagano, Japan. But that's a story that deserves its own chapter.

CHAPTER SIX

Ross Rebagliati: Olympic Gold and a Reputation Upheld

IN 1998, THE SPORT OF SNOWBOARDING WAS INTRODUCED to the world at the Winter Olympics in Nagano, Japan. Many pro snowboarders, including Norwegian superstar Terje Haakonsen, who most people accepted as the best rider in the world at the time, refused to take part.

Terje thought the contest actually represented a step back for snowboarding because snowboarders weren't in charge of it. The International Snowboarding Federation (ISF), the now defunct governing body of many of snowboarding's core events, was left out of the organizing process. Instead, it was the International Skiing Federation that moved snowboarding into the Olympics and governed how it would be run.

Two events were accepted into the big show—the half-pipe and the giant slalom. With Terje refusing to take part, a lot of the half-pipe riders felt like a shadow had been cast over the contest. Some of them, like Canadian half-pipe competitor Derek Heidt respected Terje's decision to skip the contest. "He's the best in the world and he's been that way for a long time," Heidt told the Associated

Press. "He's been very successful in the sport. If I were in his shoes and had been that successful, I would probably stand for what I believe in."

Other riders, like American Dave Downing, cast doubt on the decision, telling *Outside* magazine that perhaps Terje didn't want to compete simply because he didn't want to lose. "Say he shows up, and he wins, then what? He's already the best in the world. Why should he bother?"

The controversy surrounding the competition meant the Nagano Olympics was shaping up to be an inauspicious launch onto the global stage for the rapidly growing sport. Then something else happened.

On Sunday, February 8, 1998, Ross Rebagliati tore down the giant slalom course in his final run and won snowboarding gold for Canada. It was an amazing finish for the 26-year-old Canadian rider, and his hometown of Whistler went nuts celebrating his win. But the story of Ross Rebagliati at the Nagano Olympics didn't end on the podium. Two days later, the International Olympic Committee announced that Ross had tested positive for marijuana use and, pending an appeal, would be stripped of his medal.

While smoking marijuana is not the same as using steroids, a dark cloud had been cast over Ross' win, reminding everybody of the time Ben Johnson had tested positive for doping and lost the medal he'd won for Canada. Ross himself couldn't help but compare himself to the dishonourably discharged sprinter. He told *Maclean's*, "All I had in my head was Ben Johnson and how everyone hated him. I was ready to fly straight from Japan right to South America. I wasn't even going to come home, I was thinking, for years."

Fortunately for Ross, the fact that marijuana wasn't considered a performance-enhancing drug changed the way the media attacked the case of his infraction. While Ben Johnson's steroid use was treated as the saddest moment in Canada's sporting history, Ross' pot bust was being treated as a joke, with the blond Whistlerite's smoking run the punchline.

Ross' defence was that he hadn't actively ingested marijuana in the months leading up to the Olympics; he had simply inhaled traces of the drug at parties before leaving for Japan.

One thing working in his favour was the fact that the two Olympic snowboarding governing bodies, the International Olympic Committee and the International Ski Federation, couldn't agree on where they stood when it came to marijuana.

The job of the International Olympic Committee's anti-doping agents was to uphold the rules put in place by each sport's governing body. The International Ski Federation's rules at the time stated that, although marijuana was prohibited, severe penalties were not mandatory, but could be imposed. The Canadian Olympic Association mounted their appeal for Ross on the grounds that it was unjust that athletes, regardless of their sport, were not all treated the same.

The Canadian Olympic Association argued that stripping Ross of his gold medal would cause him far more humiliation and heartbreak than he deserved. They argued that since he had tested positive for only trace amounts of the drug and the drug in question was marijuana, not steroids or other performance-enhancing drugs, he deserved a break.

Ross issued a prepared statement to the press before the appeal. He said: "I've been training for 11 years to be the best snowboarder in the world, and that goal was achieved on February 8 in Shiga Kogen. I've worked too hard to let it slip through my fingers. I am in favour of this decision to appeal the IOC executive board's decision and will be working with the COA to prepare that appeal."

In the end, the appeal worked. The International Olympic Committee unanimously voted to return to Ross the medal he had earned for Canada on the slopes. Ross was once again a homegrown Canadian hero. He returned to Canada amid a storm of media attention. Thanks to Ross, snowboarding's introduction to the world at the Nagano Olympics was anything but quiet. Also thanks to Ross, its image as an outsider sport whose participants don't play by the normal rules remained intact. Eight years later, Ross is still a snowboarding maniac. He's planning a return to competition in time to qualify for the 2010 Olympics in his hometown of Whistler. To be sure, if Ross is there, there'll be a story to write.

CHAPTER SEVEN

Shin Campos:
Snowboard Adventurer

A Life Extreme

SHIN CAMPOS WAS BORN IN 1972 IN THE KOOTENAYS, BC. At the tender age of 14, he moved to Vancouver where he got heavily into skateboarding. It wasn't long before the youngster started hearing about the fresh new sport of snowboarding. Shin was an independent kid, always working so he'd have his own money to spend on whatever he wanted. At different times during high school, he worked as a gas station attendant, a bus boy, a fast-food cook, a caterer and a telemarketer. By the winter of 1987, he had saved enough money to buy a snowboard. He knew what he wanted. He went straight to Fairhaven Bicycles in Bellingham, Washington—one of the first places to sell snowboards in the region—and bought a swallow-tailed Burton Cruiser.

As he remembers it, the first few days were as hard as it gets. Wearing a pair of shoddy work boots, Shin tried to steer his new toy down the slope. It was no use; the thing wouldn't turn. He got going straight, but then he tumbled and came right out of his boots. Sitting there in the wet snow under the lights, Shin was tempted to give in. But the next night, he was back at it. And the next night. And the night after that. Soon, snowboarding's steep learning curve kicked in, and Shin was rocketing down the slope, turning here and there and shooting off little jumps trying to perform his favourite skateboarding tricks on the larger board.

The summer after he finished high school, Shin set off to travel around Europe with his backpack and his skateboard to spend all the money he'd saved up over the years. When he got back to Vancouver in the fall, he found out his best friends had all moved up to Whistler. There was nothing left to do but head up the Sea-to-Sky highway to find them.

By the time the first snow fell, Shin was working at the Keg Steakhouse and snowboarding the giant resorts of Whistler and Blackcomb whenever he got the chance. Before long, Shin and his friends had become a crew of young rippers ready to step up to any jump, half-pipe or slope that got in their way, and those in the business were beginning to notice.

One day during the next season, Shin got invited to go snowboarding with famed photographer Eric Berger. They did a few shoots on the hill, and then Eric invited Shin on a trip to the BC Interior with Martin Gallant. The crew hit Red Mountain in Rossland, and Whitewater in Nelson. Eric took two photos of Shin: one of him rocketing off a cliff and another of him jumping off a roof. The next season, when the pictures showed up in *Transworld Snowboarding,* Shin began to consider the possibility of an actual career doing the thing he loved most.

"Snowboarding wasn't the big thing it is now," he remembers. "Sure there were pros like Craig Kelly and Terje Haakonsen, but I never really thought I'd love to be a pro snowboarder or sponsored. But when those shots came out in the magazine, that's when I thought, well maybe...."

By the winter of 1993, Shin's third season in Whistler, he was riding more than ever and pushing himself even harder. He and his friend began competing, and at the end of that year, Shin won the overall title at the Canadian National Championships. Sponsors sought him out, and Shin accepted an offer from Luxury snowboards. By the next season, he was getting paid to ride.

Like many riders, Shin first gained recognition from the snowboard industry by winning a contest, but over the next decade he carved out a reputation as a big-mountain rider, not a competitor. Shin is constantly being invited on filming and magazine trips to the most extreme snowboarding locales because those in charge know he'll throw down at the drop of a hat. They know they can count on Shin to produce the gnarly product necessary to create a buzz in the snowboarding world. If Shin's not ripping snowmobile accessed turns within a day's drive from his home in Whistler, chances are good that he's somewhere overseas dropping a line nobody has ever even considered riding before him.

"I like going to places that are new to people, places like Bella Coola in northern BC, where there are lots of descents that are still pretty untouched." During one recent trip to the Bella Coola region with Standard films, Shin dropped into a 900-metre vertical couloir and pointed his board straight down to the bottom. The run took him a total of about 25 seconds.

"It's all pretty calculated," he says, laughing off the insanity of such feats of extreme ridiculousness. "You always check it out from the bottom, and then from the helicopter. You have your digital camera or your Polaroid, and you're taking pictures and then checking it out."

Even in the summer, Shin is often somewhere in the Southern Hemisphere or on a glacier snowboarding. If he's not snowboarding, he's mountain biking or skateboarding. Shin is dedicated to his sport, which keeps him on the edge all the time. Of course, risk is a constant factor when you choose to live the life of a snowboarder, and nobody knows this as well as Shin, who suffered a brutal knee injury in 2001 at "The Battle," a snowboard contest in Sweden.

"Right from Sweden, I was supposed to be going on a week-long, all-expenses-paid trip to Alaska," he remembers. "I tried to ride Whistler with a knee brace a couple of days before, but my knee just fell apart. It couldn't handle it, so I had to cancel that trip."

After his injury and subsequent surgery, Shin was worried about his future in snowboarding. He rehabbed well, though, and before too long he was back in top form, riding as hard as ever, pushing the limits and making tracks where most people would rather not go.

A Score to Settle

"It's time," Shin said to his friend Jon Cartwright as they rode up Whistler's Red Express chairlift.

"Time for what?" Jon replied.

Shin didn't say anything. Instead, he pointed his finger towards a giant rock face a few hundred yards up the mountain to the right of the chairlift.

"Yeah, right," Jon said smiling.

Years before, Whistler locals had named the cliff "Domanski's" after snowboarder Matt Domanski launched off it and landed in a pile. The attempt was lauded, but the cliff was deemed impossible to ride off and land. Shin wanted to land it. He'd looked at it millions of times, and he figured it was possible. Trying to ride straight off the top of the ridge was pointless. The cliff was way too big, and it would be impossible to suck up the landing with your legs. Instead, Shin wanted to sneak down a little rock ridge that ran part way down the face before going airborne and landing tighter to the bottom of the cliff.

The conditions had to be just right: lots of fresh snow and good light. Most days like that, he and his friends weren't riding the mountain resort; they were out in the backcountry on their snowmobiles avoiding the crowds and looking for fresh lines. But not today; the fresh snow from the night before was too deep and unstable for snowmobiling, so they were riding in bounds on a perfectly sunny day with more fresh snow than they'd seen all season. Shin knew if he didn't try the cliff today, he'd never try it. He got his phone out of his pocket.

An hour later, Brainwash Cinema filmer Paul Watt and photographer Dano Pendygrasse were standing at the bottom of the cliff setting up their cameras, and Shin was sitting in the powdery snow some distance from the top of the cliff, collecting himself for the task at hand. He watched as farther up the ridge an unknown hotshot dropped Whistler's most famous cliff, a double drop called Air Jordan. The crowd waiting in line at the bottom of the Peak chair cheered as he went off the first part of the cliff, and then again as he rode over the second drop, landed and cruised down into the valley.

Shin was getting impatient. He was focused, ready to go. Why did it always take them so long to set up? What if he lost his nerve? No, he was as ready as he would ever be. He felt strong, too. In his mind, there was little question he could do this. He tried to cast out all vestiges of doubt. What if he landed flat? That wasn't going to happen; he'd checked the landing so many times. He'd calculated his speed. This thing was going to get done.

Finally, he saw Paul raise his hands in the air and yell something.

"GO FOR IT!" Paul yelled.

Shin checked his bindings one more time, more out of nervous habit than anything else, and side slipped down over the powdery slope towards the edge of the ridge. He came to a small clump of trees at the top of his access point and scrambled through the two little trees nearest the edge of the cliff, keeping his weight on the toe edge of his board. A tumble now would mean a long flight into the unknown.

"Ske-tchy," he said to himself before grabbing onto the one tree he'd looked at a thousand times that would provide an anchor and allow him to lower his board onto the snow covered spine of rock below it.

A second later, his board was lined up with the ridge pointing off into the void, his hand on the tree the only thing preventing his take-off. He couldn't see the landing. It was somewhere way down over the end of the spine, maybe 20 metres below him. Launching blind like this was what made such massive cliff drops so difficult. Experience came into play simply because so much had to happen during the seconds of airtime to guarantee a solid landing. The more times you've launched a cliff, the less chance there is that your body will give up when faced with the challenge of absorbing such an impact.

Shin knew what he was in for. Still, he was nervous. If he landed on his butt, this would all have been a waste of time. He needed to ride away from this drop. It would give him a solid stunt for his upcoming video part and provide him with a bit more mileage. Worse, though, than the fear he wouldn't land it was the prospect of injury. If he did his knee in again, that was it; his career was over.

Shut up, he thought to himself. *That's not going to happen*. He was 100 percent ready.

He let go of the tree and felt his board settle onto the snowy ridge and begin to rocket towards the edge. He bent his knees and lowered his shoulders as his board rocketed down the spine of rock.

This is my job; this is what I do, Shin thought as he leapt into the void. He felt as if he was launching off the edge of the entire valley, and he was going to land in the village hundreds of metres farther down the mountain. As the air rushed passed him, he brought his knees up, grabbed the toe edge of his board and spotted the landing way down below.

The light was perfect; he could make out every contour of the snow. This felt right; he had done his homework. He was going to do this. With that final thought, his board slammed down into the snow. His knees flexed hard, he leaned forward over his feet and, like a missile exploding into flight, emerged from the puff of powder and shot down the slope. He'd landed it. He'd conquered the cliff face that had haunted his chairlift rides for years.

"YEAAAAAAAHHHHH!" his friends screamed as Shin arced a few mellow turns in the powder field below the cliff. In the distance, Shin could hear cheering coming from the chairlift. As he pulled up to where the camera crew was waiting, his phone rang in his pocket. He fished it out. "Shin! OH MY GOD! Was that you?" the voice on the other end said. It was Jon. Shin laughed.

"You know it, bro!"

CHAPTER EIGHT

Greg Todds:
The Passing of a Legend

BEFORE PIONEERING THE SPORT OF NOBOARDING, GREG Todds achieved the reputation of being one of Canada's most daring big-mountain snowboarders. Over the years, he also taught snowboarding, designed some of the best snowboard parks in the history of the sport and came up with the idea for superpipes, the oversized half-pipes commonly used in competitions. By the time he came up with noboarding, Greg had done everything he could in snowboarding. He needed a new challenge.

Instead of bindings, the noboard has a rubber traction pad and a rope fixed just in front of your front foot and just behind your back foot. The noboard is designed to be ridden in deep snow like the snow in Greg's backyard, the Selkirk Mountains around Trout Lake, BC.

"The noboard became a way for me to express my passion, because after snowboarding for so long, it got boring unless I was doing 160 kilometres an hour with my pants down," Greg told interviewer Mike Nixon at the time of the introduction of the noboard. "Getting rid of my bindings slowed me down a bit and rekindled my passion."

The noboard definitely has its advantages. As Greg put it, "It is now possible to show the world what it means to truly free-ride."

Part of the freedom noboarding affords is not having to clear snow out of your bindings and do them up at the top of the hill. With the noboard, you just grab the rope, jump on and ride, which is exactly what Greg did one fateful day while riding with a few friends in one of his favourite areas in the Selkirks.

It was the second week of January, and the riding conditions in Whistler were terrible. A huge crew from Whistler (Shin Campos, J.F. Pelchat, Benji Ritchie, Kale Stephans, photographer Colin Adair and a filmer named Dominic) decided to head out to Trout Lake to see if they could find some better snow. They loaded their snowmobiles into the backs of their trucks and headed west through the mountains.

A century ago, Trout Lake was a bustling mining centre. Now it's an all-but-forgotten backwater with a population of 20, frequented by cottagers, fishermen and of course, snowboarders. Greg was an old riding buddy of Shin's. He welcomed the chance to show Shin and the others around the backcountry slopes near his home.

When the crew arrived, the weather was only marginally better than in Whistler—socked in and snowing heavily. Still, there was plenty of snow. For the first few days, the friends rode the trees, shuttling each other up and down logging roads on their snowmobiles and riding through the deep fluff-filled stands of coniferous giants.

After a few days, the weather started to improve, and the friends decided to head up into the alpine to build a jump and try to film some riding for the next Whiteout Films Production. They packed a trail into the alpine and started building a jump. Before long, the wind started to pick up, and the temperature dropped. It wasn't meant to be. So after hitting the jump only once, the friends called it a day and headed back to their hotel in Trout Lake. The next day was supposed to be a lot nicer. They could wait.

Sure enough, the next morning the sun was high in a perfectly blue sky. It was cold and a bit windy, but the conditions were ideal for filming. After a hearty breakfast at the hotel, the crew jumped on their snowmobiles and headed up the trail to a small cabin the locals had built as a base for operations in the alpine. By the time they got up there, several of Greg's friends had arrived, but the big man himself was nowhere in sight.

The friends decided not to wait for him. They were used to Greg doing his own thing. Besides, the area was literally in his backyard. He knew where he was going. Several minutes later, the crew was at the foot of the trail they had packed the previous afternoon. The snow conditions had changed somewhat since the previous day. There was some wind loading.

After some more discussion, the crew decided to take a warm-up run down a slope called Fisher Bowl. If that went okay, they would take it from there.

"We'll stay down here in the bowl and shoot something if it looks good," Colin said.

Kale, J.F., Benji and Shin steered their snowmobiles up the trail to the top of the bowl. Guides from the CMH heli-skiing operation often brought clients to the area, and landing flags fluttered in the breeze where the crew stopped their snowmobiles. The three friends started looking for a safe way down that would still look all right if Dominic decided to film.

"I figure, air off that cornice and into the chute, and then we can straight-line, and if something happens, something breaks off, we can go right," Shin said.

Benji pointed to a line of snow-covered drop-offs that looked like marshmallows as an option.

The conversation went on for several minutes as the riders tried to decide how to attack the slope. Shin heard the sound of a snowmobile coming up behind them. He turned around just in time to see Greg pull into view.

"Hey Greg, what's going on? Where are you going?" Shin asked.

Greg mumbled something, but Shin didn't catch it. Todds jumped off his snowmobile, grabbed his noboard, and before anyone really knew what was going on, he was off down the slope. Shin turned back to the conversation with his friends. They had hardly noticed Greg come and go.

Shin didn't really think much about it at the time. *It's Greg's area*, he thought to himself. *And besides, he's probably going to stop farther down the shoulder to radio Colin and tell him he's coming down.* Shin knew Greg wanted Colin to take pictures of him riding his noboard for *Snowboard Canada* magazine. On one side of the shoulder was Fisher Bowl, where Shin and the others were planning to ride down, and on the other side were some trees. It was a broad shoulder and seemed fairly safe.

Then it happened.

A huge cloud of snow rushed to the bottom of the bowl beneath where Greg had gone down. Colin's voice came over the radio, panicky. "What's going on guys?"

"We're still here, but Greg went down the shoulder," Shin said. "Did you see Greg? Have you talked to Greg?"

It took only a second or so for the horrible realization to set in. There had just been an avalanche, Greg was missing, and it was possible he had triggered the slide and was now buried.

"GREG! GREEEEEEG!" the friends shouted. Their voices echoed in the distance, but there was no answer.

Shin sprung into action. "Okay, everyone, go to search," he said. The crew reached under their jackets and switched their avalanche beacons from transmit to search. "Benji and J.F., take your sleds down and around to the bottom of the bowl. Start searching at the end of the slide path. Kale, I'm going to strap in and go down to search where Greg went down. You follow me, but make sure I radio beforehand."

The friends sprang into action. Shin started to ride down the slope Greg had gone down, being careful not to release any new snow.

Maybe he got hung up in a tree, Shin thought to himself. *Maybe he wasn't even near the slide, and he is just around the corner.*

Then Shin saw the fracture line, and he realized without a doubt that his friend had been caught in the slide. He made his way over the slope to the top of the slide path. The going was slow as his board sank into the thick, windblown snow. Finally, he was riding down the slide path and could see Colin making his way up through the deep snow in his boots. Soon, Colin was on the massive mound of snow that had come down the mountain. It was obvious to everyone that the slide had picked up a lot of speed and had subsequently carried a lot of snow down the mountain and over some pretty rough terrain with trees on it.

"I'VE GOT SOMETHING," Colin yelled suddenly. Shin kept riding down slowly, and as he approached the spot where Colin was standing, his beacon started to beep as well.

"It's faint," Colin said. Without panicking, the friends gathered closer, trying to pinpoint the signal. Before long, they narrowed the search area down to a few square metres. They pulled out their shovels and probes and started digging, but the signal was still faint. The friends figured that Greg was buried deep in the slide, which made it much harder for them to narrow down the search area. They started digging and probing and scraping at the snow with their hands. It was hard going, and the snow kept piling back into the hole as they dug.

Finally, after several minutes, somebody probed something solid. "Here, here. I've got something. I hit something." All the shovels zeroed in on the spot, and seconds later, the crew uncovered a boot. "He's face down. Dig here. Dig here." Within seconds, they could see Greg's backpack and then his shoulders. They hauled him out onto the snow. He was bruised and blue. It didn't look good.

Shin and Kale checked Greg for vital signs, but he was not breathing and had no discernible pulse. They started to administer CPR, but before long Shin realized they were going to need professional help if they were going to save their friend.

"Benji, go get help," he said. Benji hopped on his snowmobile and shot off down the slope towards the small town. The crew was miles from any hospital. Shin knew it would take an emergency crew hours to get out to where they were. Refusing to give up, he and Kale continued to work on their friend.

A few minutes later, a helicopter rose over the trees heading straight towards them. It landed nearby and several officious-looking people jumped out carrying equipment. As it turned out, a group of doctors was heli-skiing in the vicinity. Benji had run into them during their morning warm-up run through the trees.

They ran from the helicopter to where Greg was lying.

"All right?" one of them asked Shin.

"Been better."

"How is he?"

Shin shook his head.

The new arrivals began working on Greg, relieving Shin and Kale, whose hands by this point were severely frostbitten. The doctors hooked the fallen snowboarder up to a portable vital signs unit they had brought from the helicopter.

"There's some brain activity, but it's pretty faint," one said. They bundled Greg in blankets with some heat packs, carried him to the helicopter and took off back over the trees. The friends stood in the quiet, sun-lit bowl in complete silence. The day had barely begun, but it felt like a week had passed since they had gotten on their snowmobiles that morning. They had done all they could for Greg. Now they would just have to wait for news.

After the event, Shin and the other riders reviewed it dozens of times to try to understand how they'd lost a friend. It appeared to them that Greg had ridden his noboard onto a wind slab on the leeward side of the shoulder. His weight had caused the wind slab to break off underneath him, carrying him into some trees beneath the ridge.

"It wasn't really that big, but because of all the loose snow, it gained speed and took on a lot of snow really quickly," Shin says. "It went down the skier's left side of the bowl where there's quite a lot of trees. He went down through those trees."

It turned out Greg had broken his neck during the slide. According to Shin, the fact that Greg was riding a board without bindings might have contributed to the danger of the situation.

"I definitely don't think riding a noboard made it any easier," he says. "It's harder to gain pressure on an edge. When something like a little slab avalanche or a little snow starts moving, if you put enough pressure on your edge, you can cut across stuff in its small stages. With the noboard, you're just kind of sitting on top of this board. It's super good in powder, but if you need to suddenly make a quick turn on the drop of a dime, it's going to be hard. I haven't done it much, but I can imagine."

Shin admits that the conditions that day weren't exactly safe, but it was a regular workday for him and his friends. They had recognized the danger, and at the time of the accident, they were spending time trying to find the safest descent.

"For guys like us, we definitely push the limits a little bit, but I don't know how much better we could have done except just not have been there. It's not like we're just tearing down the slope, contrary to what people think. It's not just cut and dried like that. It takes us a long time to set up a single shot."

The days following the accident were a blur for Shin. The crew headed home to Whistler to be with family and friends, but then a few days later, they headed back for Greg's funeral. The weather was terrible. Massive snowfalls, warmer temperatures and torrential rain closed roads all over BC. The friends found themselves sitting in a bar in Sycamoos with about 20 other people who had been on their way to the funeral, waiting for the road to reopen. They made it in time for the wake later that night. A few days later, determined to get back on his board, Shin headed up north on another riding trip.

It wasn't the first time Shin had encountered a tragedy. In 2000, Shin was living with his old friend Darren Proctor in Whistler. Darren was one of the original guys who had moved up to Whistler with him after high school. The two friends were always snowmobiling and snowboarding together.

One day, they were out in the backcountry with separate crews. It was a sketchy day to be out in the backcountry. The weather was iffy and the snow unstable. After several hours trying to get something together, Shin up and quit on his group.

"I was up in the backcountry in a different area [than Darren]," Shin remembers. "I had this weird feeling, and I ended up just leaving out of the blue, which is not really like me. I just left. I was over it, it was a lousy day, and it wasn't comfortable. So I left."

When he got home later that afternoon, Shin found out Darren had been swept away and killed by an avalanche while riding a nearby slope. The accident shook Shin to his core, but eventually he came to terms with what happened. Big-mountain riders like Shin have to learn to accept death as part of living and working in the mountains. Shin got back on his board and kept riding, pushing the limits. Rest assured, as you're reading this, he's probably up somewhere shredding a ridiculous line in honour of the good friends he's lost along the way.

CHAPTER NINE

Rube Goldberg:
Hard Work Pays Off

Something to Prove

RUBE STOOD AT THE TOP OF THE SHOWCASE half-pipe ON Whistler Mountain, strapped into a Nitro board on loan from The Circle snowboard shop in Whistler. He'd been playing the snowboard game for years, even placing high enough now and then to earn

Just another day at the office for Rube Goldberg, shown here throwing an inverted spin for the camera.

some money, but his nerves were still as bad as they had been that first season three years earlier when he'd started competing.

"Calm down, Rube," he told himself. "Keep it simple."

He dropped into the pipe and worked his way through his run. The board felt amazing. Rube couldn't remember ever feeling so good during a pipe run. He finished the Showcase Showdown contest in third place. On his way back down the mountain in the gondola that evening, he savoured the feeling of the $350 cheque in his hands. He felt so good, and he still had the quarter-pipe contest the next day!

The spring sun was high in the sky the following day by the time Rube found himself standing at the top of the run staring down at the giant quarter-pipe jump. The Whistler park crew had outdone themselves. The ramp, designed to shoot riders straight up into the air so they could land on the same place they took off from, was huge, but it looked perfect to Rube. A few hours later, during his final run, he shot up the huge ramp, and launched himself 5 metres into the air over the lip, grabbed his board and spun a perfect McTwist, the same move he had done the day before in the half-pipe.

The move wasn't super technical, but if he went high enough and stuck the landing, he had a good chance of winning. His board came down perfectly into the transition. Rube knew he had a good jump.

Unfortunately, due to the jump's low technical difficulty, Rube just missed the podium. He finished in fourth place and won another $250. It was a typical weekend in the life of one of Whistler's hardest working snowboarders: some good results but not good enough to earn him the attention of paying sponsors and put him on track towards the high-rolling life of the sport's top riders.

After moving out west from his hometown of Hudson, Québec, and spending four seasons riding in Whistler, Rube had accomplished a lot. He had won a ton of amateur contests—slopestyle, half-pipe and snowboardcross—and he had even made a video part for a local production company. But he still hadn't had his big break. He decided to give Nitro a call and see what they had to say about a third- and a fourth-place finish.

The guys at Nitro were suitably impressed, but they didn't have much to say. In the end, they agreed to let Rube keep the Nitro demo board for the last few weeks of the season.

A loaner board is better than what I've got in my closet, Rube thought to himself after he hung up the phone. Still, it was almost June. The season was winding down, and he had nothing to show for it except a huge Visa bill and some middling contest results. Where was that elusive break?

Finally, Something

A few days later, he got a call from Berto from Powder Mountain Snowcats in Squamish. Rube knew him because he'd taken part in some quarter-pipe contests Berto had hosted on the Brohm Ridge glacier, a wilderness area accessible only by snowmobile or snowcat.

"Mouse is coming up to film, and he needs some jumps," Berto said.

"Mouse?" Rube couldn't believe his ears.

"You heard me."

"Count me in," Rube said, his voice trembling slightly.

Rube hung up the phone and tried to catch his breath. Jamie Mosberg, aka Mouse—one of the most famous names in action sports filmmaking, responsible for snowboard titles like *Milk, Three Ring Circus*, and legendary skateboard video, *The End*—was coming to Brohm Ridge to film for his next video, *1999*, and Rube was invited. Well okay, he was being called upon to pick up a shovel and work like a slave for little or no money, but it was something. Maybe he would get a chance to pull out his board and hit some jumps. Even if there was just a slim chance of that happening, he was going to take it. He picked up the phone and started calling around.

The next day, Rube and his friends, Chris Moise, Simon Crevier and photographer Shaun Hughes drove up the long logging roads to the snowline high above Squamish where they met the snowcat for a ride to the high alpine. By noon, they were standing outside the lodge with their bags and boards in a soggy pile beside them. It was raining hard, and the mood was glum.

Rube wasn't bothered. He was looking up towards the balcony where American snowboarding superstar Tara Dakides was laughing with Canadian legend Allan Clark. The day was beginning to look a whole lot brighter.

For the next hour, the friends hung around the cabin chatting with Al, Tara and the man himself, Jamie Mosberg. Rube couldn't believe his luck. He was standing in the centre of the beating heart of the snowboarding world. Mouse was explaining what he wanted for the shoot: a massive half-pipe wall stretching 15 metres down the slope, followed by a humungous quarter-pipe, about 10 metres high, with a spine jump stretching off its left side. They tossed a few more ideas around, and the crew grabbed a bite to eat before heading back out into the rain to ride snowmobiles up to the riding zone and start digging. The crew estimated the job would take them about three days to complete. There was no time to spare.

An hour or so later, Rube was hard at work under the watchful gaze of the filmmaker from California and his henchmen. It was still pouring rain, and the snow was wet and heavy, making the job of digging the jumps grunt work of the worst order. By the end of the first day, the small crew had finished the half-pipe wall and had started work on the quarter-pipe. For the next two days, they worked their butts off, and still it continued to rain. Much of the snow melted while they worked, so they had to pile more and more snow onto their creations. It was so foggy, they could barely see what they were building. Still, they shovelled.

Finally, on the third day, the sun peeked through the fog, laying bare the monster park for all to see. "Unbelievable," Rube said, feeling a flush of pride at what they had created. "I have never seen such a beautiful hand-dug quarter-pipe."

"It's huge," Shaun said, shaking his head slowly.

As the crew added the finishing touches to the park, more professional riders who had been invited up to Brohm Ridge began to show up. As they rounded the corner on their snowmobiles, Rube could see huge smiles crease their faces beneath their goggles as they shook their heads in wonder. Helicopters buzzed up from the valley below carrying Mouse's camera equipment.

"Wow. This is the real deal," Rube muttered to himself.

Finally, an hour or so later, they were done. Rube and his friends collapsed on a nearby snowbank, cold drinks in hand, to watch as the pro riders began to session the jump. The airs got bigger as the riders adjusted to the massive transitions. The shouting among the spectators got louder as the riders upped the ante. Soon, Rube couldn't take it anymore. He grabbed his board from the snow and ran over to where Mouse was setting up some lights. Out of courtesy, he decided to ask him before dropping in.

Mouse looked up. "Sorry Rube. We've got to save this for these guys. I have to make this movie."

Rube couldn't believe it. He and his buddies had just spent the last three days building these jumps, and now the big guy was saying they couldn't ride them. It just didn't seem right. It seemed too structured. This was snowboarding, after all, not the damned PGA, or Wimbledon, or whatever.

"Screw this," Rube said, marching up to where the other riders were waiting their turn to hit the jumps. Without looking up to where he could feel Mouse's eyes watching him, Rube strapped in. "DROPPING!" he yelled, suddenly ready to take the chance he'd been waiting for so long to take. He knew the cameras weren't rolling yet, but he'd show them nonetheless.

His muscles still warm from the shovelling, Rube decided to throw caution to the wind. He shot down and threw a huge McTwist off the half-pipe wall with almost as little effort as he'd used to throw his thousandth shovelful of snow over his shoulder earlier that morning.

"SWEEEEET!" someone yelled. *Chew on that cheese, Mousey*, Rube thought to himself as he hauled down towards the quarter-pipe. Rube checked his speed slightly, worried that his legs wouldn't be able to take the compression the massive wall would dish out, but he was still going fast when he flew up the lovingly created angle. Surprisingly, he felt nothing. The jump was the smoothest he had ever taken. He launched easily 5 metres into the air and tweaked a huge backside air before plummeting back down to earth to land smoothly in the transition. Before he knew what was going on, though, he was heading straight towards the smaller spine jump to the right of the quarter-pipe and boosting a stylish frontside air before spinning to a halt dozens of metres from where Mouse was still setting up his equipment.

Rube hit the jumps with the pros for another hour before Mouse finally ended the session. He wanted to save the jumps and the riders for a night session for the cameras. Everyone headed down for a break.

Back at the lodge, everybody was excited, including Rube, who was overwhelmed by the whole situation. Maybe he had a shot at getting into Mouse's movie. That would have to lead to something big. He was so excited, he could barely eat his dinner, but the hunger brought on by three days of shovelling finally won out, and he stuffed his stomach with the gourmet feast laid out by Berto.

Afterwards, just as people were beginning to head out for the big night shred, Berto's friend Shirley from Powder Mountain Snowcats came up to Rube and asked him to follow her down to the snowline so he could bring her snowmobile back to the lodge. Rube hesitated. He couldn't refuse Shirley a favour. If it wasn't for her and Berto, he wouldn't be sitting in the lodge with a half-dozen of the best riders in the world, waiting to take part in the last big session of the millennium. "Sure," he said, somewhat reluctantly. *No big deal*, he assured himself. He probably wouldn't miss that much.

Outside, Rube could feel the air was getting cooler. He strapped on his board, and before long he was riding down, following the red light of Shirley's snowmobile over the hardening snow. It's going to be crazy hard snow on those jumps, he thought to himself. Before long, they got to Shirley's truck. She thanked Rube and gave him a big hug. "Now get up there and show those guys what you're made of," she said.

"Damn right I will," Rube said, smiling. He quickly strapped his board to the back of the sled and bombed back towards the jump zone. The sled bounced over the bumpy trail, and every once in a while Rube checked behind him to make sure his board was still there. A few minutes later, he pulled up in front of the cabin thinking maybe he would run inside and see if Tara needed a ride to the top. "Wishful thinking," he said to himself, smiling as he hopped off the sled, but when he looked to where he had strapped on his board, it was gone.

He couldn't believe his eyes. Rube immediately ran back down the trail in the direction he had just come from. As he ran farther away from the lodge's lights, the trail grew darker, and he could hardly see in front of him. He ran back to the sled, jumped on, gunned the engine, spun around and headed the machine back down the trail.

I can't have lost it, he thought to himself. *It's impossible. Not now! NO WAY!* Rube gunned it down the trail, bouncing over the hardening snow. "Don't crash," he said, slowing up somewhat, realizing he was going way too fast. For the next hour, Rube drove up and down the trail looking for the board. Finally, he gave up. It was gone, the night session was probably over, and he felt like the biggest loser in the world.

"Some break," he said, choking back huge feelings of self-pity. He was so frustrated, he felt like crying, but after a few minutes, he gathered himself together and drove up to catch what was left of the session.

When he got there the spotlights were shining bright, and the jumps looked like a great big fantastical snow fort. Rube staggered over to Berto. "Get your ass up there, bro!" Berto said jovially. Rube could feel his lips starting to quiver. "I lost my board in the woods, and now I have nothing," he said, his voice catching slightly. Berto, who had followed Rube's snowboarding career like a father, sensed the sorrow of the moment and passed his friend a beer without saying a word.

After watching for a while, Rube began to feel a little better. With the cooler air, the jumps were getting much harder. *I probably would have killed myself anyways*, he thought.

Most of the riders were taking it easy, knowing the conditions were too dangerous to try much. Before long, it was all over, and everyone headed back to the lodge to celebrate. All anybody could talk about was how amazing the quarter-pipe was. Soon, Rube had forgotten about the lost board and started to feel good about being part of it all again.

The following day everyone went back to hit the jumps one last time, and Tara showed everyone why she was considered the world's best female freestyle snowboarder at the time. Rube took a few runs on Kale's board, but he couldn't put anything together. He had just gotten too used to the Nitro board.

"When I got home, I had to break the news to the Nitro rep about his board, and I had to shell out $150," Rube remembers. "Fortunately for me, Nitro ended up hooking me up later that summer, and it made it all worth while."

Sometimes luck is on your side. Other times not. Rube, who has a particular penchant for poker, day trading and other games of chance, was used to the feeling of a lucky break turning unlucky. But in spite of all the whoop-de-doos on Rube's chosen life trail, he was soon making a name for himself in snowboarding. The next spring, he finally got the break he was looking for, but it had less to do with luck and more to do with his growing ability to blow minds with his jumps.

Rube Goldberg shows the kids at summer camp on Mt. Hood how to ride a half-pipe.

A Classic Move

By the time the Westbeach Classic rolled around in April 2000, Rube was more than ready to throw down. The contest had mellowed out quite a lot since 1998, when Kevin Sansalone took home the gold in the big air contest. His victory had come at the bottom of the mountain, under the lights, in front of a huge drunken crowd. This contest was being held at the top of the hill during daylight. The format was much the same, though, with the riders first jumping to qualify and then having a couple of chances to impress the judges during the finals.

The previous day, Rube had killed it in the half-pipe contest, qualifying in first place and finishing in fifth. Although he didn't have a huge sack of tricks for the big air, he went into the contest riding a wave of confidence.

As the time for his first jump in the finals approached, Rube found himself sitting in the snow wondering what the heck he was going to do to impress the judges enough to win some money. He had time for one more practice jump, he figured, so he dropped in and wound up for another 720. "Go big," he told himself as he shot over the sun-soaked spring snow towards the jump. He threw himself into the air and grabbed his board, spinning first one revolution and then another before plopping down onto the landing. The crowd cheered. There was no question—he had this jump dialled in.

Snowmobiles were ferrying the riders back to the starting area, and Rube was waiting with Kevin Sansalone for a ride. He didn't know Kevin very well at that point, but he knew that the North Vancouverite was on top of his game. Since winning the Westbeach Classic Big Air contest in 1998, he'd won gold at the X-Games Big Air and silver at the Gravity Games Big Air. That day on the top of Whistler, Sansalone was again blowing minds with his huge inverted spins.

"Nice jump," he said to Rube.

"Thanks," Rube said.

"But you can't do that anymore."

Rube looked up. "What do you mean?"

"You've gotta do something different," Kevin said.

"I don't have a huge bag of tricks," Rube said, kicking at the snow between his feet.

"Doesn't matter. You've gotta do something. Go bigger. You've gotta change it up if you want it to go anywhere."

Kevin has what it takes to win contests, Rube thought to himself. *If he says I need to switch it up, I need to switch it up*. Suddenly, it dawned on Rube what he had to do.

"What are you planning?" the starting official asked when it was time for Rube's run.

"Backside 180."

"That's it?"

"That's it."

It was a simple trick, a trick he and every other serious snowboarder probably does a dozen times on any given day on the mountain, but Rube was going to take this simple trick into the stratosphere. He was going to forsake technical difficulty for sheer guts. He wasn't going to check his speed. He was going to launch as high as he could and throw in a "Japan" grab for good measure, a tricky move that requires good flexibility and confidence in the air.

Rube shot off the lip of the jump going faster than anybody had gone so far that day. The jump was massive. He grabbed his board and held on, floating slowly so his butt was towards the landing. He soared over the place where most of the other riders had landed and just before he touched down, he rotated his board the last few degrees to land backwards. The crowd went nuts, surprised to see such a simple move during a contest that was basically a spinning symposium.

"THAT WAS INSAAAAAAAANE!" the announcer screamed over the loudspeakers. "A huge backside 180 from Rube Goldberg." Rube took off his board and waved all around at the crowd around the landing area. He spotted his friend Mike Hart over in the stands and went over to join him.

A few minutes later, Rube heard a stranger behind them talking about his jump. "I can't believe it," the voice said. "I think that guy might have just won the contest with a backside 180!"

Had Rube won? It was impossible. This was the biggest contest on the calendar in Whistler. There were a lot of big name riders there, although not as many as in past years. *Don't get too excited*, Rube told himself. After all, Kevin still had to jump.

A few minutes later, Kevin stormed down and cranked off a huge inverted switch rodeo 720. *This contest is over*, Rube thought to himself. He was happy for Kevin, but unhappy because he knew that no matter how big he went with his simple jump, it could never measure up against the technical wizardry of Kevin's jump. Finally, they announced the results. Rube finished in second place, just behind Kevin. His friends cheered ecstatically as he went up to claim his $1500 cheque.

"I was definitely pretty pumped," Rube says, remembering that day. "I remember going to bed that night thinking, this could be the beginning of my career, for sure."

Days later, Rube got on the phone to Nitro and started working out his first pro deal. It didn't happen over night, but Rube eventually quit his job delivering pizza and started pulling in enough money from his riding to make ends meet. A few solid video parts, a few great photographs and an interview or so later, Rube was a bona-fide pro snowboarder, moving in the same circles as the guys he had looked up to as a young rider growing up in Québec. All his hard work had finally paid off.

Pushing the Envelope

Over the years, Rube's ability to throw down insane tricks under pressure has grown. Still, snowboarders are constantly upping the stakes, and no rider is immune to dangerous situations, at least not if they want to stay in the game.

One of Rube's most intense experiences occurred the day he went snowboarding with an old filmer friend named Rick—the brains behind Brainwash Cinema—for his latest snowboard movie aptly titled, *BAMM!!*

It was the first day of the season, and Rick wanted the crew, including Rube, to head into the backcountry, find something big and launch some seriously crazy jumps.

"We can't just keep hitting the same jumps year after year," Rick told his young crew. "We need to go big. We need to stand out from the rest".

Rider Tyeson Carmody had seen a huge step-down jump in the backcountry. They decided to start with that. They woke up bright and early, jumped on their snowmobiles and headed up to the spot. The trail was super-bumpy and long, and by the time the riders got to the site, they were exhausted from muscling their sleds through the rough terrain.

From the bottom, the jump looked to be about a 12-metre drop over a bunch of rocks, with at least a 6-metre gap to clear beforehand. Rube could feel his legs begin to wobble just imagining flying down towards it.

"It's on!" he shouted, doubting the sincerity of his valiant call to arms. The crew parked the sleds and made their way to the top of the gap to start building a cheese-wedge shaped jump to launch them over the space. Before long, the jump was finished, and it was time to start the throw down.

"All right," Rick said looking around at his crew of riders. "Who's going first?"

Nobody spoke up. Jumping into powder is an art that takes practice. It was the first session of the season, and many of the riders hadn't launched anything significant into powder since the previous spring. Many of them could hardly remember the feeling of landing on their feet in deep snow. None of them was too excited about assuming the role of guinea pig for the experiment.

"Somebody's gotta go," Rick said after a while.

"I'll do it. It's my jump," Tyeson said suddenly, grabbing his board and making his way to the starting point.

"Three...two...one...DROPPING!"

Rick's camera rolled as Tyeson barrelled down the take-off towards the jump. He took off looking good in the air. Then he disappeared over the crest of the landing. Did he land it? Eric Greene, who was standing so he could see the landing, shook his head and smiled.

Rube was next. He hiked up to where Tyeson had started his run. "It's like I'm dropping off the edge of the world," he said, shaking his head. Still, what choice did he have? He had to step up. This was no joke, after all. A good jump here would guarantee a good opener for his part in the video. Tyeson hadn't landed it. The jump was his to claim.

Rube gave Rick the heads up over the radio. "All right, I'm dropping," he said. There was no turning back now. He gunned towards the take-off. *I'll spin a frontside 540*, he thought to himself, seconds before launching into space. He'd gone way too big. The frontside 540 soon became a 720, and finally Rube was spinning completely out of control, his arms flailing in the air. The landing still seemed a mile away as he floated through the sky.

Then....

BAMM!!

There was a flash of light.

He landed with a thud in the powdery snow. His arm went numb and his face filled with blood. After rag dolling down the slope, Rube finally came to rest. He flexed his toes in his boots, then his fingers. "I'm okay," he said quietly to himself. "All systems go, all systems go." Rick's face suddenly loomed up in front of his snow-covered goggles. "Rube," he said. "That was seriously the most insane thing I've ever seen. You were like, a hundred feet in the air."

"I fell out of the sky and landed on my face," Rube said, wiping blood from his lips with his glove. He raised his head and looked back up the slope to see where he had landed. "Yup. I'd say that was a little big."

Rube wasn't badly hurt—he had some bruises on his arm, a black eye and a sore nose—but he sat out the rest of the day to watch his friends assault the jump. No one went quite as big as he had, and no one landed anything. The jump was a man-eater, no doubt about it. It appeared as though the Brainwash crew had bitten off slightly more than they could chew. They decided to name the gap, the Brainwash Gap, after Rick's fledgling company. "I still haven't been back to seek revenge on the jump, but that effort definitely opened some more doors," Rube recalls smiling.

CHAPTER TEN

Risto Scott: Finding Fame and Flirting with Disaster

FOR SOME SNOWBOARDERS, GETTING SPONSORED AND becoming a professional takes years of hard work and dedication. For others, like Risto Scott from Kelowna, BC, the process is much more straight-forward: ride for a couple of years at your home

Flips, spins or flipped spins, Risto Scott knows how to get gnarly on his snowboard.

mountain, move to a mecca of snowboarding such as Whistler, win a contest and wait for the cheques to start rolling in.

Risto followed his friend, skier Mike Passmore, to Whistler in the fall of 1994. "I moved there for something to do," Risto remembers. "I'd been living in Kelowna for a couple of years, working at a restaurant and snowboarding, and I was kind of getting ready to do something else. So I moved to Whistler."

"I think in the back of my head, part of me was saying, I wonder if I can make a go of this? Get sponsored. Originally, it was just going to be for a year. That's what everyone says."

Risto arrived in Whistler and dove headfirst into the burgeoning snowboard scene. In the evenings, he worked at a restaurant in the Delta Hotel, and during the day, he and his friends sessioned the Wind Lip on Blackcomb, probably one of the most famous natural jumps in snowboarding. The Wind Lip is basically a giant snowdrift that forms every season in the same place in the alpine zone at the top of Blackcomb. Risto and his friends spent hours there every day flying off the massive jump and landing in the soft snow, before hiking up for another turn. They worked hard perfecting their tricks and pushing the envelope of aerial mastery. Fun drove them and fed their need to improve. Visions of a life as a professional snowboarder were buried deep in their minds, if they existed at all.

Soon, it was almost the end of the season. The Kokanee beer company announced it was hosting a giant big air contest on Blackcomb, and Risto and his friends decided to register.

"I was super nervous," Risto recalls. "I remember registering, and Al Clark and all these pros were signing up, and I was thinking to myself, 'Oh My God. What am I getting myself into?'"

The jump loomed massively over the slope, and Risto prepared himself for disappointment in front of the large crowd of spectators. It was the early days of crazy spinning tricks, and Risto had just perfected a new move called a Cab 900—launching off the jump backwards, spinning two and a half times and landing forwards. Would he be able to pull it off here, in front of all these people, on an unfamiliar jump, with more pressure than he had ever felt? There was only one way to find out, and that was to try.

Risto warmed up with a couple of easier spins in practice, but as the finals got underway, and he felt he had a good understanding of the jump he was competing on, he decided he had no choice. He had to try the Cab 900.

"Up next, we have Risto Scott from Kelowna. Risto is riding for…. Actually, Risto has no sponsors," the announcer said. "Here he comes now! Heads up, folks!"

Risto shot into the air above the giant wedge and started to spin. He grabbed his board strongly as he soared through the air. A second later, he cruised down onto the landing. Perfect.

"RISTO SCOTT! Ladies and Gentleman! With a Cab 900, the first today." The crowd was cheering madly for the unknown talent. He'd done it. He'd pulled the Cab 900. He still had one more jump, but he knew the one he'd just done was good enough to at least place him near the top of the field. Forty-five minutes later, it was Risto's turn again, and he decided to try the trick he'd perfected on the Wind Lip once again.

"ANOTHER PERFECT CAB 900! WHO IS THIS GUY?" screamed the announcer. Risto couldn't believe it. He suddenly realized that the hours he'd spent having fun with his friends that season had actually been practice for a bona-fide sport. He'd been practicing to become a better snowboarder, and judging from the noise coming from the crowd, he'd accomplished exactly that. An hour or so later, feeling slightly bewildered, Risto hopped onto the podium to accept his first-place cheque.

"From there, I had so many different offers," he recalls. "I could pick and choose between different sponsors. That was the turning point."

Meanwhile, Risto was still hitting the hill with his friends, working at the restaurant and carrying on with his life, until one day he suffered an injury that threatened to put an end to the fairytale adventure he was embarked on.

An Extremely Close Call

It was the summer after the Kokanee Big Air contest, and one of Risto's friends, Kris Elliot, was visiting from Kelowna. The friends had decided to enter a big air contest on the Blackcomb Glacier. Kris went first in the contest and pulled an incredible jump, worthy of the top prize. Risto could hardly believe his eyes. How was he going to top that? He and Kris had always been fiercely competitive, so he knew he had to do something crazy. Still, he hadn't felt comfortable on the jump all day. Should he just say forget it, do something mellow and hand the win to his friend? No way, he had to go for it.

Risto bombed down towards the jump. "YEE-HAAA!" he shouted as he tore towards the tabletop. As he shot up the take-off ramp, he suddenly knew he had way too much speed. It was too late, though; he was already committed to a backside rotation. Just as his board left the jump, his edge dug into the soft spring snow, sending him into the air sideways. Risto flew through the air, completely out of control, and soared right over the landing ramp. His body began tipping upside down in the air. Almost 15 metres past the landing, he came crashing down onto the run on his upper shoulders and neck. Knocked unconscious and barely breathing, Risto was air-vaced to the Vancouver General Hospital's spinal unit.

After several days in critical condition, Risto woke up.

"When I finally got up and walked around, I noticed there were six or seven other people in the spinal chord unit," he remembers. "They told me I was the only one who was ever going to walk again."

Risto had broken his neck to within a quarter of a millimetre of his spinal cord. He had come very close to joining the ranks of those less-fortunate victims surrounding him in the ward. He'd gotten lucky, no doubt about it. The injury took him out for the rest of the summer, but by late August, he was healthy enough to take his first trip abroad, to Argentina, as a professional snowboarder.

The Business of Riding

Risto's win at the Kokanee Big Air had paid off in spades. Faster than he could say, "I can't afford my rent," Risto was receiving what he and his friends called "Free Money" from his sponsors in the mail.

"The first couple of years was kind of like a honeymoon," he remembers. "I just partied, and every month or so a cheque would show up. My friends Khris Elliot and Brad Baxter moved up and it was a joke. Every day we'd check the mail, and if there was a cheque, we'd basically go straight to the bar and blow it all."

By the next season, Risto had quit his day job and had started snowboarding full time. He entered a lot of contests but soon realized that his sponsors were more than happy to simply let him ride, in hopes of getting good photographs for the magazines or decent footage for the latest film. Whistler photographer Dano Pendygrasse stepped in and gave Risto a leg-up into the spotlight. "He was instrumental in getting me going," Risto says. "He worked with me before I really had a name."

For the next 10 years, Risto parlayed his snowboarding skills into a living. It wasn't all smooth sailing though. Many times over, he paid the price for living a life on the edge. While filming for a Whitey Productions film called *Revival*, Risto blew out his shoulder, and not long after that, he landed on a rock and broke one of his vertebrae. After a while, the cycle of injury, recovery, injury, recovery started to wear on Risto, and snowboarding began to feel more like a job than the fun pastime it had once been. He began to explore other options. In 2003, he completed a marketing and communications program at the British Columbia Institute of Technology

"I liked the snowboarding industry, and I wanted to stay involved in it," he says. "Then the Billabong team manager called me and asked me if I would be interested in working for them. They wanted to create a position for me."

Now, Risto is the marketing manager for Billabong Canada. He's also the team manager for Billabong's wakeboard, skateboard, snowboard and surf teams. Now he's the one handing out free money to those he thinks deserve it. The game has changed a lot in the last few years, but it's a lot easier for him to relate to the up-and-coming talent than someone who's never played the game before.

"I've never regretted quitting snowboarding," Risto insists. "I mean, sometimes when I'm in the office and there's a foot of fresh powder, I might think about it. But definitely, it was a good life decision for me to make."

Notes on Sources

Note: Most of the information for this book came from the author's own interviews with the riders.

Anderson, Peter. "Rube Goldberg (Price is Right)." *Snowboard Canada*, Winter, 2004: 132–140.

Bethel, Greig. "Boarders got a break at Baker: Sport got its start in 1985 with race at 'The Chute'." *The Province*, February 5, 2004: A31.

Boyer, Jon. "Kevin Sansalone Ain't Gonna Tend No Chickens." *Transworld Snowboarding*, October 1999. www.transworldsnowboarding.com

Crane, Lee. "Shin Campos: The Interview." *Transworld Snowboarding*, February, 1997. www.transworldsnowboarding.com.

Duhatschek, Eric. "Rebagliati loses gold medal to marijuana." *The Province*, February 11, 1998: A3.

Falcon, Mike. "North Vancouver's Kevin Sansalone is Canada's king of... Big Air." *The Province*, December 6, 2001: B4.

Greenfeld, Karl Taro. "Adjustment in Midflight." *Outside Magazine*, February, 1999. www.outside.away.com.

Hudson, Dan. "A conversation with rider Kevin Sansalone." *Calgary Herald*, March 8, 2002: E3.

Hunter, Stuart. "Duct tape for the soul: Annual Mt. Baker event reminds snowboarders of the good old days." *The Province*, February 3, 2000: A52.

Jones, Terry. "Wasted on the way. Smoking out a snowboarder is hardly Ben Johnson material." *Edmonton Sun*, February 11, 1998: www.canoe.ca

Kingston, Gary. "Snow is her magic carpet." *Vancouver Sun*, January 8, 2005: F3.

Makepeace, Brad. "Feature: Risto Scott." *Transworld Snowboarding*, February, 2001. www.transworldsnowboarding.com.

Mike and James. "Seymour's chairmen of the board." *The Province*, January 7, 2001: B7.

Nixon, Mike. "Life, Death, Progression—The Greg Todds Profile." *Biglines.com*, February 17, 2005. www.biglines.com.

O'Leary, Jim. "D-Day Thursday for Rebagliati." *SLAM! Sports*, February 11, 1998: www.canoe.ca/SlamNaganoSnowboarding.

Pelchat, J.F., Nicholas Royer. "Etienne Gilbert." *Snowboard Canada*, Spring, 2003: 184–190.

Polischuk, Darrin. "Victoria Jealouse: Focused on taking charge." *Calgary Herald*, November 28, 2001: S7.

Rebagliati, Ross. "Statement to the Press." Wednesday, February 11, 1998. www.canoe.ca/SlamNaganoSnowboarding.

Ricker, Maëlle. "Canadian Snowboard Team gets its first look at Olympic venues." *Pique Newsmagazine*, February 17, 2005.

Simmons, Steve. "Ross goofed but so did the IOC." February 11, 1998. www.canoe.ca/SlamNaganoColumns.

Taylor, Derek. Victoria Jealouse Interview. www.powdermag.com

Walker, Ian. "Boarding hero hits the slopes: Ross Rebagliati plans return to competition." *Vancouver Sun*, April 15, 2005: G1.

"Check Out: Risto Scott." *Transworld Snowboarding*, October, 1999. www.transworldsnowboarding.com

"Family cheers historic victory: Whistler snowboarder wins first Olympic gold." *The Vancouver Sun*, February 9, 1998: A1.

"Gregory Richard Todds, 1971–2005." Obituary. www.noboard.ca

"Police to Question Banned Canadian athlete on drug use." Reuters-CP, February 11. 1998: www.canoe.ca.

"Sled Heads." *Transworld Snowboarding*, November, 2000: www.transworldingsnowboarding.com

Tom Peacock

Tom Peacock is a freelance journalist and writer living in Montréal, Québec. He began writing at *The Ubyssey* student newspaper at the University of British Columbia and has since worked as a reporter for the *Sherbrooke Record* and as a regular contributor to *Verge* magazine. One winter many years ago he tried snowboarding just once, and he was hooked and learned all that he could learn about it. When he's not out on the slopes or writing, Tom can be found at Radio Canada International working as a production assistant.